Trauma Kit Haiti

Healing the Wounds of Trauma
Human Questions and God's Response
When Someone You Love Dies
God's Peace, My Peace
Someone I Love Died

David C Cook

Provided free to Christian Leaders in Haiti by David C. Cook

TRAUMA KIT FOR HAITI
Published by David C. Cook
4050 Lee Vance View
Colorado Springs, CO 80918 U.S.A.

David C. Cook Distribution Canada
55 Woodslee Avenue, Paris, Ontario, Canada N3L 3E5

David C. Cook U.K., Kingsway Communications
Eastbourne, East Sussex BN23 6NT English

David C. Cook and the graphic circle C logo are registered trademarks of
Cook Communications Ministries

This kit is available through David C. Cook in English and Haitian Creole.

ISBN: 978-1-4347-0235-7

The Team

Design and illustration: Scott Johnson, BMB Design

Haitian Creole translators: Jean Killick Aristide & Marie Nehemie Aristide

Reviewed for best practices in trauma counseling by Janet McCormack, D.Min., B.C.C. and
Heather Davediuk Gingrich, Ph.D., both from Denver Seminary, Colorado U.S.A.

Resource Expert: Dr. Dieumeme Noelliste, Vice Chairman of the Board of STEP (Seminary of
Evangelical Theology of Port-au-Prince) and professor of Theological Ethics, Denver Seminary

Printed in the United States of America
First Edition 2010

1 2 3 4 5 6 7 8 9 10

122109

*Dedicated to Pastors and Christian
leaders in Haiti.
Our prayer is that God will
use you to bring spiritual and
emotional healing to earthquake victims.*

About This Trauma Kit

There are five different pieces in this kit. Each has a different use.

- Flip through the kit and note that there is a tab on the right side of the first page of each of the five parts of this kit.

- Each part of the kit starts with the page number 1.

- Each page is perforated. This will make it easy to tear out sections and give them to people who will use them.

- You have permission to photocopy each section for free so that more than one person in your church can use the material. All parts of the kit must be given away free.

The 5 Different Pieces in This Trauma Kit

1. HEALING the wounds of TRAUMA—How the Church Can Help

This 11-session curriculum guides pastors and leaders through the helping process—their own and the people God wants them to serve. This part of the kit has been adapted for Haiti by David C. Cook from the original curriculum developed by Wycliffe Africa. It is designed to be used in a group.

2. When You Lose Someone You Love—Comfort for Those Who Grieve

This is a case study built around the letters a pastor writes to Jean, a Christian man who lost his beloved wife in the earthquake. Pastors and church leaders will gain an intimate understanding of the struggles grieving Christians go through. Ideally two people should read this section at the same time, and discuss it together. Together they determine how it can be best used in their church.

3. Human Questions and God's Response—A Scripture Guide for Church Leaders

This guide provides assistance to pastors and lay leaders who minister to those who have been touched by the January earthquake. Biblical principles address questions for which there are no simple answers. It is designed to be studied and referred to often when difficult questions arise.

For Children

4. God's Peace, My Peace—Trusting God in Terrifying Times

This activity-based lesson will help children ages 4 to 10 replace their fears with peace. A prayer walk will get children in touch with Jesus, as they share their emotions with him. The lesson is designed to be used by a parent with his or her child, or with groups of children in a Sunday school or orphanage.

For Children

5. Someone I Love Died

This interactive children's book is to be read by the child or with a parent. The child will have an opportunity to draw his or her thoughts and feelings. Through art therapy, the child learns to talk honestly with God and understand that God never gets angry when a child shares real feelings, even when they include anger and pain and hurt.

Margaret Hill, Harriet Hill, Richard Baggé, Pat Miersma

HEALING
the wounds of
TRAUMA
in Haiti

*How the
Church
Can Help*

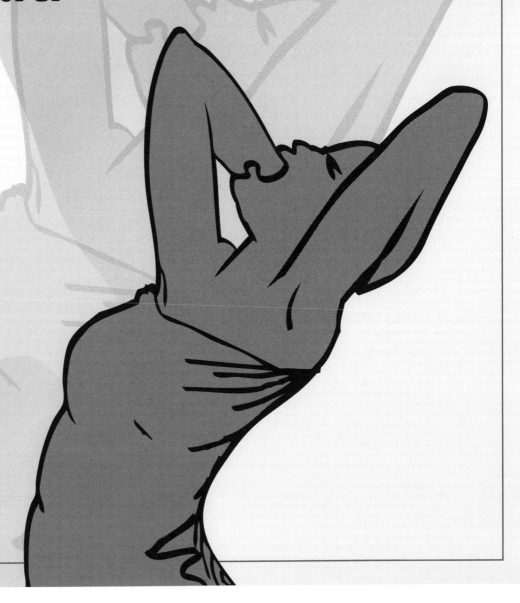

Margaret Hill, Harriet Hill,
Richard Baggé, Pat Miersma

Healing the Wounds of Trauma in Haiti
How the Church Can Help

David C. Cook with permission of Wycliffe Africa

This Haitian edition is provided free to Pastors and Church Leaders by David C. Cook.
David C. Cook, 4050 Lee Vance View, Colorado Springs, CO 80918 U.S.A.
Haitian Edition: 2010

HEALING THE WOUNDS OF TRAUMA © Wycliffe Africa, P.O. Box 44456, Nairobi 00100 Kenya
ISBN 9966-21-792-4. Year of publication: 2004; 1st reprint: 2005; Revised edition: 2007.

HEALING THE WOUNDS OF TRAUMA
©Wycliffe Africa, P.O. Box 4456, Nairobi 00100 Kenya
ISBN: 9966-21-792-4
Year of first publication 2004
1st Reprint 2005
Revised edition 2007
Haiti edition 2010

Scripture quotations are taken from the Good News Bible © American Bible Society.

Typesetting and Layout of the original book by Mukundi Miringu

Typesetting and Layout of the Haitian editions in English and Creole
by Scott Johnson, BMB Design

Editor for Haiti editions: Randy Petersen

Haitian translators for Creole edition: Jean Killick Aristide & Marie Nehemie Aristide

Reviewed for best practices for pastors and lay-Christians by Janet McCormack, D.Min., B.C.C.
and Heather Davediuk Gingrich, Ph.D., both professors at Denver Seminary, Colorado U.S.A.

Haiti Resource Expert: Dr. Dieumeme Noelliste, Vice Chairman of the Board of STEP (Seminary
of Evangelical Theology of Port-au-Prince). The school in Port-au-Prince was destroyed in
the earthquake and one student died. Dr. Noelliste is professor of Theological Ethics, Denver
Seminary, Colorado U.S.A.

Cover Design by Lawrence Mbugua

Haitian editions printed in the U.S.A.

David C. Cook expresses a debt of gratitude to Wycliffe Africa for giving permission to develop a Haitian edition in both Creole and English of *Healing the Wounds of Trauma.* This tool for healing is provided free to pastors and church leaders through donations of Christians in the United States, England and Canada to David C. Cook.

This section of the Trauma Kit is addressed to people who have experienced some kind of trauma, such as earthquakes and other natural disasters, as well as war and criminal activity. This edition particularly seeks to help church leaders who have members in their churches, adults and children, who have been traumatized by the devastation of the January 2010 earthquake in Haiti. The chapters deal with different aspects of trauma, giving basic physiological teaching within a biblical framework.

People can understand and experience God's healing best in their own heart language. Because of this, the book was originally written in a style of English that is easy to translate into other languages, such as Haitian Creole.

This book was conceived and developed during a series of workshops for church leaders from countries experiencing conflicts. All four authors are members of Wycliffe International. Dr. Richard Baggé is a psychiatrist and Pat Miersma a professional counselor. Dr. Harriet Hill and Margaret Hill are *Scripture Use* consultants.

CONTENTS

DEDICATED
To the Church in Haiti

"The LORD is near to those who are discouraged;
he saves those who have lost all hope."
(Psalms 34:18)

ACKNOWLEDGEMENTS

This book was inspired by Rhiannon Lloyd and Kristine Bresser's book, *Healing the Wounds of Ethnic Conflict: the Role of the Church in Healing, Forgiveness and Reconciliation* (printed in 1998, unpublished). Ideas from that book are used with the author's permission, and that of Mercy Ministries International, CP 442, 1215 Geneva 15, Switzerland.

These materials were first used in the Ngbaka community in Northwest DRC. They were then revised and expanded at a workshop sponsored by the Institute for the Study of African Realities, May 2001. Participants at that workshop came from East African countries that had experienced trauma and war. Other participants had expertise in trauma healing: Karl Dortzbach *(Institute for the Study of African Realities)*, Joyce Fiodembo *(Counselor, Nairobi)*, Emmie Gichinga *(Counselor at GEM Counseling Services)*, Violette Nyrarukundo *(Counselor, Kigali)* Anastasse Sabamungu *(Coordinator, AEE Trauma Healing Programme, Kigali)*.

At a second workshop in March 2002, the materials were taught to pastors from six war-torn areas in Africa, and translated into their mother tongues. These participants led local workshops using the materials, and reported back at a third workshop in April 2003. The materials were further refined and are now ready for wider use, including use in Haiti. We acknowledge the help of Cindy Langermann and Kathie Watters at these workshops, as well as artwork from Joyce Hyde, SIL International.

Scripture quotations are taken from the Good News Bible ©American Bible Society.

INTRODUCTION

In many parts of the world today, wars, ethnic conflict and civil disturbances, crime and natural disasters have left people traumatized. Often those traumatized are Christians, and the church has a clear responsibility to care for them. Beyond the church, Christians are to be light and salt in the world. This is particularly important in times of conflict and suffering.

The Scriptures are included throughout this book because it is the knowledge of God, his character and his relationship to people that are the foundation for healing. There are many places in the Bible that speak of his people suffering. For example, suffering is one of the main themes in certain epistles. The Psalmists are able to express how they feel in times of suffering. The whole book of Job treats the problem of innocent people suffering.

This book seeks to help church leaders who are called upon to help members in their congregations after major trauma has occurred. These traumas can include among other things, actions committed during war, criminal activity, and traumas as a result of natural disasters such as earthquakes, floods, landslides, and storms. These things may happen to whole communities, to families or to individuals. Though this book focuses on events happening to entire communities related to the earthquake, the same principles can be used in helping people in other difficulties. The book will also help individuals who are struggling with the issues surrounding suffering. The information in each lesson gives basic counseling principles within a biblical framework.

God's Word speaks most deeply to people in the language of their hearts. The intention of the authors of this book is that it be translated into the language of the people where it is used, and that the Scriptures in the local language be used.

HOW TO USE THIS BOOK

This book is normally intended as a textbook for seminars. Leaders from all the churches in the area should be included in these seminars, if possible. The highest church leaders should be taught first, and then they can teach others who can in turn teach others (2 Timothy 2:2). In this way, the teaching can permeate an area.

Lessons 1, 2, 3, and 9 are the core lessons, and should be taught at all seminars. Lesson 1 discusses the questions about God that come when there is great suffering. Lesson 2 helps us to recognize that wounds of the heart need to be cared for, in the same way that physical wounds need to be cared for. Lesson 3 describes the process of grief that allows us to be healed from trauma and loss. Lessons 4–7 cover special topics that may be important for your community: helping children who have experienced trauma, helping people who have been raped, ministering in the midst of AIDS, and caring for the caregiver. Choose the lessons that are most important for your community according to the time you have available.

"Taking Your Pain to the Cross" (Lesson 8) provides a special time for people to experience God's healing of their pain in a very meaningful way. It is often done in an evening session, towards the end of the seminar.

Lesson 9 is a core lesson. It should be done after "Taking Your Pain to the Cross." It deals with forgiveness and repentance. If your community is torn by ethnic tension, continue with Lesson 10, which is on living as a Christian in the midst of ethnic tension. All seminars should close with the Final Ceremony which provides participants with an opportunity to confess their sins and receive God's forgiveness.

LESSONS	RESPONSE
Core: Lessons 1, 2, 3	
Optional: 4, 5, 6, 7	
	8 Taking Your Response to the Cross
Core: Lesson 9	
Optional: 10	
	Final Ceremony

Another important part of the seminars is to have participants share the trauma they have experienced. They should do this without justifying themselves, accusing others, or giving too many details that might frighten others. (Remind the participants that it is completely up to them as to if, what, and how much they choose to share.) The group can then pray for those who have shared. This brings healing and bonds the group together in a special way. It is often done in evening sessions. Be careful about privacy issues. People should not share anyone's story outside of this group without the person's permission. If they want others outside of the group to pray for concerns that were raised, they should ask for prayer in generic terms only; the name and details of those who shared should not be given without permission.

Seminars may last from three days to a whole week or more. The whole book cannot usually be taught in one seminar. Take time to cover the topics well. Subsequent seminars can be arranged to cover the rest of the book and to discuss experiences participants have had teaching the materials to others.

You might not have time to cover everything in a lesson. Study the lesson in advance, and pick the teaching and exercises that seem most relevant for your situation. Feel free to change the names or details in the stories to make them more appropriate for your situation. You may need to prepare skits or gather materials for certain lessons. Lesson 8 and the Final Ceremony require special preparation of materials before you begin. Instructions are found at the beginning of those lessons.

The lessons should be translated into the local language in advance. If possible participants should receive copies, especially if they will be teaching the materials to others.

Participants should bring the Scriptures they have in the local language with them to the seminar. Take time to look up the Scripture references that are in the lessons and read them out loud. Some are printed directly in the sessions. It is the Word of God that gives life and will feed people's souls. If participants are not used to looking up passages, leaders may need to give instruction on how to do this. This will be time well spent. You may want to give out the references for a lesson on slips of paper to participants before the lesson begins, so that they can find them in advance and be ready to read them without delay during the lesson. If people do not have a copy of the Scriptures you are using, write the passages out on a blackboard or on a large piece of paper.

People learn best by participation, and for this reason these lessons are not supposed to be given as sermons. Section titles are often in the form of questions. Ask the group to answer the question. Then add any points from the book they have not mentioned. There are many exercises included. These should be done by all participants for the full value of the book to be realized. People remember 20 percent of what they hear, 50 percent of what they see, and 80 percent of what they experience. They will learn more if the leaders lecture less.

Each lesson starts with a story set in Haiti that depicts the problem the lesson addresses. These stories should be read aloud. Then there is the teaching of the lesson. Interspersed throughout the lesson are questions to be discussed in small groups. The purpose of these questions is to get the participants thinking about the subject and sharing their ideas. Their responses should be heard and understood, without elaborating on them. As you teach the materials, you can then reinforce what they have said, correct it, or add to it. Each lesson ends with a closing exercise.

Discussion can be done either as a large group, in small groups of three or more, or in groups of two. Vary the kinds of groups you use throughout a lesson. The small groups allow more participation by more people, especially those who are quiet in the large group. Each group can report a summary of their discussion back to the large group. Since it takes time for people to get into small groups, save these for longer exercises. Groups of two are faster to organize. People can just talk with the person next to them. Generally, groups of two do not report back to the main group. Use these for shorter questions. Remember, participation is key to good learning. (Due to the intense emotions associated with Crisis and trauma, participants should be allowed to opt out of anything that proves too difficult for them. You might want to assign a few leaders to watch for those who are overcome by the lessons and assignments. These observers could then take any distraught person aside for private counsel.)

Lesson 1

IF GOD LOVES US, WHY DO WE SUFFER?

1. The Story of Pastor Andre

When Andre was three years old, his father died and he went to live with his uncle. His uncle was cruel to him, beating him often and not letting him have enough to eat.

Andre grew up and through help from another family member was able to go to school. He became a Christian and knew that Jesus had died for him. In time he had the opportunity to go to Bible school and became the pastor of a small country church. Over the following years, Andre saw many bad things: government officials taking bribes, rich people treating poor people like dirt, and even a hurricane that devastated the land. Eventually, Andre felt called by God to serve a church in Port-au-Prince. There, he felt he might truly make a difference. An opportunity arose, so Andre and his family moved to the big city. But there he found the problems were even worse.

When the earthquake hit, he was teaching a class on the second floor of the church building. It totally collapsed. Bruised, he was still able to walk to safety. Others were trapped in the rubble. Pastor Andre was a strong leader in those first few hours, and in the next few weeks. He put together rescue teams and made sure the church people shared food and water with those who needed it.

But today, in his heart he is confused and angry. Andre keeps asking why God has let this suffering happen to his people. He is angry with God and feels that God has deserted him. Sometimes he thinks that maybe God is not strong enough to prevent these things from happening. Sometimes he thinks that maybe these terrible things have happened because of the sin of his people, and this makes him preach more about the judgment of God. When Andre preaches about God's love, he often feels like a hypocrite, because he really feels God is far away.

 DISCUSSION QUESTIONS

1. What is Andre feeling in his heart about God?

2. Why do you think Andre feels this way about God?

3. Have you ever felt like Andre?

2. Is the God of the Bible Different from Our Culture's View of God or of Pastor Andre's View When He's in the Middle of the Crisis?

 DISCUSSION QUESTION

In our traditions, what do people believe God is like? Did he create the world? Did he then go away and leave it?

Cultures, like people, are not perfect. They shape our beliefs, but need to be evaluated in the light of Scripture so that they can be corrected and redeemed. People's personal theology is often tested in a crisis as they try to make meaning out of their experiences. Meaning will often be a process, rather than stagnant as people continue to try to integrate their theology with their experiences and their culture.

 SMALL GROUP DISCUSSION

For each of the following verses, discuss these questions.

1. What do these verses teach us about God's character and his relationship to us?

2. How is this similar or different from our traditional view of God?

Psalms 91:14,15. Because he loves me, says the Lord, I will rescue him; I will protect him, for he acknowledges my name. He will call upon me, and I will answer him; I will be with him in trouble. I will deliver him and honor him.

Matthew 9:35-36. Jesus went through all the towns and villages, teaching in their synagogues, preaching the good news of the kingdom and healing every disease and sickness. When he saw the crowds, he had compassion on them, because they were harassed and helpless, like sheep without a shepherd.

1 Peter 5:7. Cast all your anxiety on him because he cares for you.

1 John 4:9-10. This is how God showed his love among us: He sent his one and only Son into the world that we might live through him. This is love: not that we loved God, but that he loved us and sent his Son as an atoning sacrifice for our sins.

Psalms 103:2-5,11-14. Praise the Lord, O my soul, and forget not all his benefits—who forgives all your sins and heals all your diseases, who redeems your life from the pit and crowns you with love and compassion, who satisfies your desires with good things so that your youth is renewed like the eagle's. For as high as the heavens are above the earth, so great is his love for those who fear him; as far as the east is from the west, so far has he removed our transgressions from us. As a father has compassion on his children, so the Lord has compassion on those who fear him; for he knows how we are formed, he remembers that we are dust.

Exodus 34:6,7. And he passed in front of Moses, proclaiming, "The Lord, the Lord, the compassionate and gracious God, slow to anger, abounding in love and faithfulness, maintaining love to thousands, and forgiving wickedness, rebellion and sin. Yet he does not leave the guilty unpunished; he punishes the children and their children for the sin of the fathers to the third and fourth generation.

3. When We Are Suffering What Do We Need to Remember about God's Character?

A. Read Romans 8:35-39 aloud:

"Who, then, can separate us from the love of Christ? Can trouble do it, or hardship or persecution or hunger or poverty or danger or death? As the scripture says,

"For your sake we are in danger of death at all times; we are treated like sheep that are going to be slaughtered.

No, in all these things we have complete victory through him who loved us! For I am certain that nothing can separate us from his love: neither death nor life, neither angels nor other heavenly rulers or powers, neither the present nor the future, neither the world above nor the world below – there is nothing in all creation that will ever be able to separate us from the love of God which is ours through Christ Jesus our Lord."

 DISCUSSION QUESTION

What can we learn about God's character in times of suffering from this passage?

Sometimes when trouble comes we think it means that God doesn't love us anymore. This is not true. Nothing can separate us from his love. God promises to always be with us, even when we suffer (Psalms 23:4-5; Hebrews 13:5b-6; Isaiah 43:1-2).

God still loves us.

B. Read 2 Peter 3:9-10 aloud:

"The Lord is not slow to do what he has promised, as some think. Instead, he is patient with you, because he does not want anyone to be destroyed, but wants all to turn away from their sins. But the Day of the Lord will come like a thief. On that Day the heavens will disappear with a shrill noise, the heavenly bodies will burn up and be destroyed, and the earth with everything in it will vanish."

 DISCUSSION QUESTION

What can we learn about God's character in times of suffering from this passage?

When we pray that God will stop a certain evil thing, and it continues, we must not think it is because God is weak. He is in control and hears our prayers. He is slow to act because he wants to give everyone time to repent, not because he is weak. When the time is right, he will powerfully judge sin (Psalms 73:25-28; Romans 9:22-24).

God is all-powerful.

C. Read Psalms 34:18 aloud:

"The LORD is near to those who are discouraged; he saves those who have lost all hope."

DISCUSSION QUESTION

What can we learn about God's character in times of suffering from this verse?

Jesus understands our suffering because he suffered on the cross. His suffering was far beyond anything we will ever experience (Matthew 27:46; Hebrews 12:2-3). He suffers with those who are suffering (Matthew 25:35-36). He is merciful and gracious even when we have doubts (Isaiah 63:9; Isaiah 53:3-4; Hebrews 2:18).

God suffers with us and feels our pain.

D. Read Genesis 6:5-6 aloud:

> "When the LORD saw how wicked everyone on earth was and how evil their thoughts were all the time, he was sorry that he had ever made them and put them on the earth."

DISCUSSION QUESTION

What can we learn about God's character in times of suffering from this passage?

Not everything that happens is the perfect will of God. God hates evil and injustice (Proverbs 6:16-19; Romans 1:18).

God hates evil and injustice.

4. Why Is There Suffering in the World?

DISCUSSION QUESTION

Why do people think there is suffering in the world?

The Scriptures tell us:

A. Sin entered the world when Adam and Eve disobeyed God.

Adam and Eve are the ancestors of all people. When they disobeyed God, evil and death entered the world (Genesis 3:1-24). All people, Christians and non-Christians, experience the effects of Adam and Eve's disobedience (Romans 5:12).

B. Satan has rebelled against God and tries to get us to rebel.

Satan rebelled against God, and he wants to get as many people and spirits as he can to rebel against God with him (Luke 22:31; 1 Peter 5:8-9). He is a liar and murderer (John 8:44). Those who obey him lie, kill, and destroy.

C. God gives us freedom to choose whether we will obey him or not.

God created all people with the freedom to choose good or evil (Matthew 7:13). He is grieved when we choose to do bad things, but he does not stop us (Matthew 23:37b).

Sometimes, even though we obey God, we suffer because of other people's evil choices (1 Peter 3:14-17).

5. How Does God Use Suffering?

God's word teaches us:

A. God uses suffering to purify our faith.

When gold is heated over a very hot fire, the bits of dirt in it rise to the top. These can be skimmed off, leaving the pure gold. Suffering is like fire: it is painful, but it results in purifying our faith in God (1 Peter 1:6-7; James 1:2-4). It makes us yearn for God's kingdom (Romans 8:18; 2 Corinthians 4:16-18; Romans 5:3-5; 1 Peter 3:14-17).

God's love is stronger than any suffering. In terrible situations when everything else is taken from us, we can experience the fact that God's grace is all we really need (2 Corinthians 12:9-10).

B. God turns evil into good.

Joseph's brothers sold him into slavery, but God used this experience to deliver the Israelites from famine (Genesis 50:18-20).

God turned the greatest evil that was ever done into the greatest good for us all when Jesus was crucified on the cross (Acts 3:13-15; Philippians 2:8-11). God works in ways we don't always understand, but we can always trust his character (Romans 8:28; 11:33-36). In the end, Satan will be completely defeated (Revelations 20:10).

C. God comforts us in our suffering so we can comfort others.

God comforts us when we suffer. He holds us in his arms (Isaiah 40:11). He comforts us with his Word (Psalm 119:50, 92). We can pass on this same comfort to others when they suffer (2 Corinthians 1:3-5).

 SMALL GROUP DISCUSSION

Share how God has used suffering in your lives, perhaps in one of the ways mentioned above.

6. Why Is It Difficult to Believe in God's Goodness When We Suffer?

A. Childhood experiences can sometimes make it difficult to believe in God's goodness.

Children need to feel secure and protected from evil. If we have experienced difficult things as a child, we may find it difficult to trust others or God when we become adults. For example, if we grew up without a father or mother, or if our father was often angry with us, then it might be hard for us to believe that our heavenly Father loves us. The Bible teaches us that God is a loving Father (John 17:24; Romans 8:14-17).

A Loving Father

 **DISCUSSION IN TWOS**

Think about your own father. As a child, did you experience your father's love? How does your experience with your earthly father effect your experience with your heavenly Father?

B. Some sermons make it difficult to believe in God's goodness.

i. Sermons that dwell on God's anger and judgment.

Sometimes churches teach a lot about how God judges us when we sin, but not much about how he loves us. It is true that God is all powerful, but we must also remember his great love for us (Jeremiah 31:3; Lamentations 3:22-23; 1 John 4:9-10).

ii. Sermons that teach that we are saved by what we do.

Another dangerous teaching is that each person has to live a good life before that person can please God or be used by him. We may think we are suffering because we haven't been good enough to please God. God's love is not based on our behavior. He loved us before we turned to him (Romans 5:8; Titus 3:4-5; 1 John 4:19). He continues loving us by grace, not because of what we do (Romans 3:23-24; Ephesians 2:8-9).

iii. Sermons that promise prosperity for everyone who believes.

A teaching called "The Prosperity Gospel" says that if we obey God, we will always be rich and healthy. When people suffer, this teaching will make them feel guilty, because people will say they have caused their own suffering. The Apostle Paul is a good example of someone who suffered a lot even though he was very obedient to God (2 Corinthians 1:8-10).

C. It is difficult to remember God's goodness when we do not do the things that will help our faith grow strong.

As we follow Jesus and study the Bible, we learn the truth about God and this sets us free from the lies of Satan (John 8:31-32; 2 Timothy 3:14-17). Christians need to meet together for teaching, prayer, and fellowship (Acts 2:42; Philippians 4:6-7; Hebrews 10:24-25). If these things are missing, we will find it much harder to believe in God's goodness when we suffer.

D. The church does not speak out against evil and injustice.

God put the church in the world to challenge injustice and to help those in need (Luke 4:18-19; Matthew 25:31-46). When the church does not do its work, evil increases, and people lose hope that God is really good like the Bible says.

 **SMALL GROUP EXERCISE**

We have talked about six things that make it difficult for us to believe in God's goodness when we suffer:

- *Childhood experiences*

- *Sermons about God's judgment*

- *Sermons about being saved by what we do*

- *The "prosperity gospel"*

- *Not doing things that keep us strong*

- *Church not speaking out against evil*

Which of these factors might keep you from believing in God's goodness when you go through suffering?

CLOSING EXERCISE

1. Experience God's love:

> *a. Have everyone close their eyes and listen while someone slowly reads these verses.*

Lamentations 3:21-23. Yet this I call to mind and therefore I have hope: Because of the Lord's great love we are not consumed, for his compassions never fail. They are new every morning; great is your faithfulness.

Psalms 103:13-14. As a father has compassion on his children, so the Lord has compassion on those who fear him; for he knows how we are formed, he remembers that we are dust.

Romans 8:14-16. Because those who are led by the Spirit of God are sons of God. For you did not receive a spirit that makes you a slave again to fear, but you received the Spirit of Sonship. And by him we cry, 'Abba, Father.' The Spirit himself testifies with our spirit that we are God's children, then we are heirs—heirs of God and co-heirs with Christ, if indeed we share in his sufferings in order that we may also share in his glory.

1 John 3:1-2. How great is the love the Father has lavished on us, that we should be called children of God! And that is what we are! The reason the world does not know us is that it did not know him.

1 John 4:9-10. This is how God showed his love among us: He sent his one and only Son into the world that we might live through him. This is love: not that we loved God, but that he loved us and sent his Son as an atoning sacrifice for our sins.

1 Peter 5:7. Cast all your anxiety on him because he cares for you.

> b. *Inspect your heart. Do you have any hidden doubts about God's love? If so, tell them to him.*

> c. *Think about God as your loving father. In your mind, imagine you are a child with your loving father. Sense the love in his eyes as he looks at you.*

> d. *Sing some songs about God's love for us. You may even make up new songs.*

2. *Divide into small groups. Have each group make up a skit about one of the following topics:*

> a. *Adam and Eve sinning (Genesis 3).*

> b. *God's frustration with people choosing to do evil before the flood (Genesis 6).*

> c. *Joseph meeting his brothers and explaining how God used their evil for good (Genesis 50).*

> d. *A child with an unloving father being taken into a new family with a loving father.*

> e. *Someone helping a person who has experienced suffering overcome their incorrect thoughts about God.*

Lesson 2

HOW CAN THE WOUNDS OF OUR HEARTS BE HEALED?

1. The Story of Jean and Marie

Jean and his wife Marie lost their home in the earthquake. They had an adult son, Ti-Jean, living with them, who worked as a teacher at a school run by their church. Fortunately Jean was the only one at home when the quake hit. A wall fell on top of him, crushing his arm. Marie and Ti-Jean arrived in time to dig him out, but it was a week before Jean could get medical attention, and then his arm had to be amputated.

As life slowly came back to normal, Jean did his best to function with only one arm, but he knew that even if the factory where he worked opened again, he couldn't do his job anymore. The whole family, now living in a tent in the public square, pitched in to earn any money they could, but it was very hard. Jean seemed to be angry with everyone. He started beating his wife, and quarreling with all the neighbors. Marie was not angry with people but she felt very sad inside. She wasn't interested in eating very much, and often thought about dying. Sometimes when she was alone, she became very frightened for no particular reason. Both she and Jean had trouble sleeping and often had nightmares.

The son, Ti-Jean, who had been a very good teacher, drank a lot with his friends at night. He had a lot of headaches and stomach aches, but the clinic couldn't find anything wrong with him.

All three of these people were Christians and went to church regularly. Now, they met in the open area in front of the church because they feared the building was unstable. Every Sunday the pastor preached about hope and renewal. One day, Marie began telling the pastor's wife how miserable and frightened she felt, but the pastor's wife told her that Christians should not have feelings like that. This made her feel ashamed of her feelings, so she never tried to talk about them again.

Jean's friends never talked about his missing arm. They just pretended nothing had happened. But his whole life had changed! He could not pretend that nothing had happened. However, Jean believed that men shouldn't talk about their problems, so he kept his feelings inside. Ti-Jean did the same.

 DISCUSSION QUESTIONS

1. What wounds are Jean, Marie, and their son carrying, in addition to Jean's physical wound?

2. In our area, what are some ways in which people's hearts have been wounded?

3. What does our culture teach us to do with our emotions when we are suffering inside?

2. What Is a Wound of the Heart?

A. A heart wound is like a physical wound.

 DISCUSSION QUESTIONS

Think of a deep cut on a leg: How does it heal? What helps it heal? How is a wound of the heart like a physical wound?

The first column to the right describes a physical wound. The second column describes a wounded heart. Both kinds of wounds need to be treated for healing to occur.

If possible write this chart on a blackboard or on a large piece of paper.

PHYSICAL WOUND	HEART WOUND
It is visible.	It is invisible, but shows up in the person's behavior.
It is painful, and must be treated with care.	It is painful, and must be treated with care.
If ignored, it is likely to get worse.	If ignored, it is likely to get worse.
It must be cleaned to remove any foreign objects or dirt.	The pain has to come out, and any sin must be confessed.
If the wound heals on the surface with infection still inside, it will cause the person to become very sick.	If people pretend their emotional wounds are healed when really they are not, or if they ignore them, it will cause the person greater problems.
Only God can bring healing, but he often uses people and medicine to do so.	Only God can bring healing, but he often uses people and an understanding of how our emotions heal to do so.
If not treated, it attracts flies.	If not treated, it attracts sin.
It takes time to heal.	It takes time to heal.
A healed wound leaves a scar.	A healed heart wound also leaves a scar. People can be healed, but they will not be exactly the same as before the wound.

B. How do people with wounded hearts behave?

 DISCUSSION QUESTIONS

Can you think of some people in your church or around you who are showing unusual behavior because they have bad wounds in their hearts? How do they act?

Some people with wounded hearts are always tense. Every loud noise makes them jump. They are frightened all the time, and expect another bad thing to happen at any moment. They may be so tense they can't fall asleep, or they may wake up very early. At times, they may shake or have a fast or irregular heart beat. At other times, they may have difficulty breathing, or feel dizzy or faint. Some people with wounded hearts are very angry, hateful, and can become violent. For example, women who have been raped may be angry at all men or even at God who, they feel, let it happen.

Some people with wounded hearts are very sad and depressed and may cry a lot. They may avoid people, even family they were close to.

Some people with wounded hearts may avoid anything that brings back memories of traumatic events they have experienced. For instance, earthquake survivors may jump when they feel a large truck rumbling past. Some people who have been hurt by Christians may refuse to go to church.

Some people with wounded hearts may not be able to remember part or all of what happened to them.

Some people with wounded hearts feel numb. They don't care very much what happens to them. They have no energy. They are no longer disturbed by violence or seeing dead bodies. Sometimes they stare at nothing.

Many people with wounded hearts find themselves thinking about the event all the time. At times, they may feel they are back in the event, re-living it. This can happen while they are awake or in their dreams, as nightmares. Thinking about the event all the time will make it hard for them to concentrate on a particular task. For example, school children may find studying difficult.

Some people with wounded hearts may tell everyone about what has happened over and over again. On the other hand, some people may refuse to talk about it at all.

Some people with wounded hearts may try to kill the pain by taking drugs or alcohol. Others may eat too much or work too much as a way to avoid feeling the pain.

All these reactions are normal in people who have been through bad things like a devastating earthquake. These reactions may happen immediately, or may be delayed and start happening a long time after the event.

C. What makes some wounds of the heart more serious?

Some situations are more difficult than others. The two hardest traumas to deal with are 1) the death of a child, and 2) the death of someone just like you in job or age or anything else the person identifies with. Here are other things that make the wounds very serious:

- Something very personal, for example, a family member dying or being betrayed by a close friend.
- Something that goes on for a long time.
- Something that happens many times over a period of time.
- Something connected with death.
- Something that people have done intentionally to cause pain rather than something that is accidental.

One person who has experienced a smaller trauma may react more severely to it than another person who has had a bigger trauma. The "feeling" about the smaller trauma may be the same "feeling" from a past trauma, even if it's not the same type of event. A person is likely to react more severely to trauma if that person is already:

- Someone who always is used to someone else telling him or her what to do.

- Someone who has mental illness or emotional problems.

- Someone who is naturally rather sad, or who is sensitive.

- Someone who had many bad things happen in the past, particularly if they happened when he or she was a child, like both parents dying.

- Someone who already had many problems before this happened.

- Someone who did not have the support of family or friends during and after the event.

3. What Does the Bible Teach Us about How To Handle Our Feelings?

Some Christians who have troubles like this say that we shouldn't think or talk about our feelings. They also say that we shouldn't go to others for help with our troubles. They say we should just forget the past and move on. They think that feeling pain in our hearts means we are doubting God's promises.

A. Biblical characters share their feelings.

 DISCUSSION QUESTION

What do these verses teach about handling our emotions?

(Jesus) Matthew 26:37-38 He took Peter and the two sons of Zebedee along with him, and he began to be sorrowful and troubled. Then he said to them, "My soul is overwhelmed with sorrow to the point of death. Stay here and keep watch with me."

(Jesus) John 11:33-35 When Jesus saw her weeping, and the Jews who had come along with her also weeping, he was deeply moved in spirit and troubled. 'Where have you laid him?' he asked. 'Come and see, Lord,' they replied. Jesus wept.

(Peter) Matthew 26:75 Then Peter remembered the word Jesus had spoken: "Before the rooster crows, you will disown me three times." And he went outside and wept bitterly.

(Hannah) 1 Samuel 1:10, 13-16 In bitterness of soul Hannah wept much and prayed to the Lord. Hannah was praying in her heart, and her lips were moving but her voice was not heard. Eli thought she was drunk and said to her, "How long will you keep on getting drunk? Get rid of your wine." "Not so, my lord," Hannah replied, "I am a woman who is deeply troubled. I have not been drinking wine or beer; I was pouring out my soul to the Lord. Do not take your servant for a wicked woman; I have been praying here out of my great anguish and grief."

(Jonah) Jonah 4:3 Now, O Lord, take away my life, for it is better for me to die than to live.

Jesus had strong feelings and shared them with his disciples. The Bible is full of examples of people pouring out their hearts to God: for example, Hannah, David, Solomon, Jeremiah. The Psalmist tells us that if we hold our pain in, it can make us sick. "When I kept silent, my bones wasted away through my groaning all day long" (Psalms 32:3 NIV). God wants us to be honest and speak the truth from our hearts. Paul teaches us to share our problems with each other as a way of caring for each other (Galatians 6:2; Philippians 2:4).

B. Laments

In Psalms 13:1 David says, "How long, O Lord? Will you forget me forever?" In verses 5 and 6, he says, "I have trusted in thy steadfast love; my heart shall rejoice in thy salvation. I will sing to the Lord, because he has dealt bountifully with me." How can he say both of these things at the same time? They seem contradictory.

One kind of Psalm is a lament Psalm. In a lament, people pour out their complaints to God in an effort to persuade him to act on their behalf, all the while stating their trust in him.[1] Laments can have seven parts:

1. Address to God (O God)

2. Review of God's faithfulness in the past

3. The complaint

4. A confession of sin or claim of innocence

5. A request for help

6. God's response (often not stated)

7. A vow to praise, statement of trust in God

Not all parts are present in each lament, and they are not always in the same order. Laments allow people to fully express their grief, and even accuse God,

[1] (Sixty-seven of the Psalms are considered laments – more than any other type of Psalms. Some were for use by individuals; others were used by the community together. The individual lament Psalms are: 3, 4, 5, 6, 7, 9-10, 11, 13, 16, 17, 22, 25, 26, 27, 28, 31, 35, 36, 38, 39, 40, 42-43, 51, 52, 54, 55, 56, 57, 59, 61, 62, 63, 64, 69, 70, 71, 77, 86, 88, 94, 102, 109, 120, 130, 140, 141, 142, 143. The community lament Psalms are: 12, 14, 44, 53, 58, 60, 74, 79, 80, 83, 85, 90, 106, 108, 123, 126, 137.)

but this is followed by a statement of trust in God. This combination makes for very powerful prayers. The grief is not hidden, but the person does not stay in his or her grief – the person calls on God and expresses faith in him. The laments encourage people to be honest with God, to speak the truth about their feelings and doubts. When they do, he can act.

In a lament, people do not attempt to solve the problem themselves, but they cry to God for help. They look to God, not the enemy, or in a situation like an earthquake, they look to God as the one ultimately in control of the situation. They ask God to take action to bring justice rather than taking action themselves or cursing the enemy (Psalms 28:3-4).

 EXERCISES

1. Read Psalms 13 together in class. Identify the parts of this lament.

vs. 1-2 How much longer will you forget me, LORD? Forever? How much longer will you hide yourself from me? How long must I endure trouble? How long will sorrow fill my heart day and night? How long will my enemies triumph over me?	Address and complaint
vs. 3-4: Look at me, O LORD my God, and answer me. Restore my strength; don't let me die. Don't let my enemies say, "We have defeated him." Don't let them gloat over my downfall.	Request
vs. 5a: I rely on your constant love;	Statement of trust in God
vs. 5b-6: I will be glad, because you will rescue me. I will sing to you, O LORD, because you have been good to me.	Vow to praise

2. Laments are well known in many ethnic groups. They are a very good way to express deep emotions. Compose a lament in your mother tongue about your own painful experiences. It may be a written lament, a song, or a song and dance. Share your lament with the group.

4. How Can We Help Someone Heal from the Wounds of Their Heart?

 **EXERCISE**

Do a skit that shows someone listening well to another person, and one that shows someone not listening well. Discuss what you observed.

People get pain out of their hearts by talking about it. Usually people need to talk to another person about their pain before they are ready to talk to God about it. If they are able to talk about their bad experiences, then after a while their reactions will become less and less. But if people are not able to talk about their pain, and if there is no one to help them, these severe reactions may continue for months and even years. They may get worse as time goes on rather than better.

This talking can be done one on one or in a small group. The group should not be more than ten or twelve people, so that everyone has a chance to speak. The group could be a married couple, a family, or people who experienced a painful event together. If some people do not want to talk about their problems, they can be invited to listen. In time, they may be ready to share, too.

It's important to find a safe and quiet place so that people can talk freely. Babies and small children should be cared for so parents can talk without being distracted by them. The group will probably need to meet more than once.

A. What is the goal of letting people talk about their pain?

By giving people the opportunity to talk about their pain, they can:

- Gain an honest understanding of what happened and how it has affected them (John 8:32).
- Accept what happened.
- Be able to trust God, rest in him, and let him heal them (Psalms 62:8; 103:3).

B. What is a good listener like?

 DISCUSSION QUESTION

What kind of person would you feel free to share your deep pain with?

For people to feel free to share the deep wounds of their hearts, they need to know that the person:

- Cares about them.
- Will keep the information confidential (Proverbs 11:13).
- Will not criticize them or give them quick solutions (Proverbs 18:13).
- Will listen and understand their pain.

Pastors can identify wise and caring people and train them for this ministry. The hurt person should be allowed to choose who he or she feels at ease talking to.

C. How can we listen?

The listener should let the speaker speak at his/her own pace. It may take several meetings before the whole story has been discussed.

The following questions may help the listener guide the person into telling their story:

- What happened?
- What were you doing when it happened?
- What were you thinking?
- How did you feel?
- What was the hardest part for you?
- What gave you strength and helped you to get through it?
- How did God help you?
- How were you able to help others?

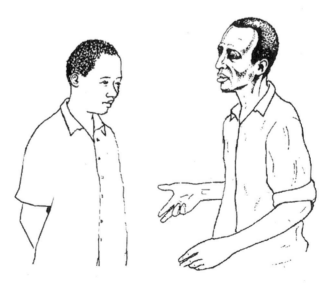

Show you are listening by responding in appropriate ways. This may be by looking at them, or by saying words of agreement like "Mmm" or "please tell me more." Don't look out the window or at your watch. Don't seem impatient for them to finish. Don't tell them what they should think or feel or do. It is important to be sensitive to cultural concerns as you listen. For example, eye contact when listening or speaking may or may not be appropriate in some cultures.

From time to time, repeat what you think the person has said. This gives the person a chance to correct, restate or affirm your understanding.

If the person remembers dreams, encourage him or her to talk about them, and what the person thinks they mean. This may be their inner self working through the event while the person is asleep. It may also be God speaking to the person in his or her pain. The meaning of dreams is symbolic. The things that happen in dreams should not be taken as if they occurred in real life. The person may need to tell the dream, or what he or she thinks it means, over more than once. Commit any distressing dreams to the Lord in prayer.

When the person is ready, pray for him or her. Eventually, people need to bring their pain to the Lord themselves, but it will take time for them to be ready to do so.

D. Serious cases.

People who are very wounded may need more help than you are able to give them by listening to their pain. To evaluate how seriously people have been wounded, look at:

- How many problems they have in the ways they behave (see Section 2C).
- How frequent the problems are.
- How intense the problems are.
- How many months or more the problems last.
- If the problems keep them from taking care of themselves and their families or get in the way of their being able to work.

People who are seriously wounded need professional help. If a psychologist or psychiatrist is not available, an ordinary doctor or nurse may at least give them medicine to calm them down and help them sleep.

✕ CLOSING EXERCISE (1 HOUR)

Divide the participants into groups of two. Each person in turn tells about one hard, hurtful or difficult thing that has happened – a small event rather than something very big. The other person listens. The listener must be careful to listen properly and to show he or she has understood, and is sharing in the speaker's pain. The listener should use the questions suggested in section 4C. After ten minutes, switch roles. In a large group discuss:

• How did you feel during this exercise?

• Was anything difficult?

• Did you feel heard when you were listened to? Why or why not?

• What did the listener do well?

Lesson 3
WHAT HAPPENS WHEN SOMEONE IS GRIEVING?

1. The Story of Pastor Leon

The church building was in ruins, but Pastor Leon knew the real church lived on. As night fell on the terrible day of the quake, people found their way to the place where the church had been and they shared their stories. Weeping turned into singing. With candles in hand, people lifted their voices in the familiar hymns of faith.

In the days and weeks that followed, the people continued to meet there, day and night. Some men managed to pull a few of the old wooden pews out of the rubble and set them up in the street. Services went on as before, but in the open air. Many church members had been lost in the quake, and others were injured, but there were also new people attending.

But as time went on, Leon became very concerned about the emotional state of some of the Christians in his church. Some of the adults who had lost family members were very sad and wouldn't try to find work, or even help to find food. They seemed to have lost interest in life in general. One man kept saying over and over again, "If only I had reached for the medicine before I ran out of the house, my wife would be alive today!" One woman who had lost her husband was repeatedly telling everyone that she could hear her husband speaking to her. Another woman insisted that her son had not died even though everyone had seen his dead body. She kept expecting him to show up at church. Pastor Leon realized that, without official funeral ceremonies for the many who had died, their friends and families had trouble accepting the fact that they were really gone.

Often Leon himself had really bad nightmares and woke up crying out for his wife. He was also angry inside. He wanted to be strong in front of his people, to be an example of faith, so he tried to hide his true feelings. But privately he had to admit that he was angry with God for allowing this catastrophe. He was also angry with the government for its inefficiency, with the builders for shoddy home construction, and with the gangs of looters in the streets. When Leon heard about one shop owner who pulled a gun and shot a looter, he almost wished he could have been the one pulling the trigger. Because he couldn't show this anger openly, it was burning him inside.

 DISCUSSION QUESTIONS

1. What is Leon experiencing?

2. Have you ever felt like Leon?

2. What Is Grieving?

Grieving is mourning the loss of something. This might be the loss of a family member or a friend. It might be the loss of a body part or the function of part of the body. It might be the loss of property or position. Whether small or enormous, all losses affect us and make us experience some degree of grieving.

When people lose someone or something very important to them, they may lose their sense of who they are. This is particularly true when a child or spouse dies, or when someone loses a part of their body or sight. Through the grieving process, a person's old sense of who he or she is changes and adjusts to the new way of life. This takes time.

Grieving is part of the normal process of recovering from a loss. Only in heaven will there be no more crying (Revelation 21:4). Because Christians have the hope of heaven, when they grieve they do not despair like non-Christians do (I Thessalonians 4:13). They are sad, but they are not afraid.

3. How Can We Grieve in a Way that Brings Healing?

Grieving takes time and energy. It is like a journey that takes us through several villages.

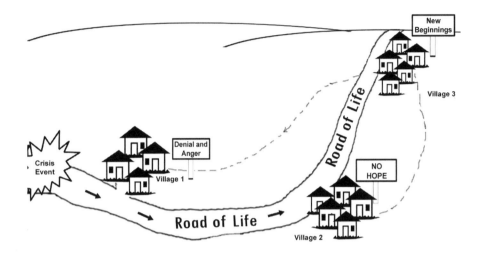

The Journey of Grief

A. The Village of Denial and Anger.

Village 1 is the Village of Denial and Anger. Just after people experience a loss, they are often numb and not completely aware of what is happening around them. They can't believe that the person has really died, or that the event actually happened. At other moments they may suddenly start to cry or erupt in anger. They may be angry with God, or with the person who has died for leaving them alone. They may have many questions such as, "If only I had done this or that, he wouldn't have died," or, "I wish I had . . ." Or, "Why did it happen to me?" A person may also be tempted to find someone to blame for the death, and may try to take revenge. This often results in conflict and broken relationships which increase the pain.

Sometimes people refuse to believe that the person is really dead. They think that the person is still there. Often people dream of seeing or hearing the dead person. This happens to people all around the world, and is not necessarily connected with evil spirits.

This stage may last for a month or longer after the loss. The weeping and rituals of the wake and burial are helpful ways of accepting the reality of the loved one's death. In situations where there is no funeral, it's even harder to move past denial.

 DISCUSSION IN TWOS

Think of a loss you have experienced. Did you have any of these feelings?

B. The Village of No Hope.

Village 2 is called the Village of No Hope. When people get to this village, they often feel sad and hopeless. They might find it hard to organize their lives. They still continue to long for the dead person to come back. They may feel very lonely and neglected and may even think about killing themselves. It is possible that they may feel guilty—as though it was their fault the person died, or as though they are guilty for having lived when someone else died (Survivor's Guilt)—even when there is no reason for this. The questions that started in Village 1 may continue.

Often people stay in this Village of No Hope for 6-15 months.

C. The Village of New Beginnings.

Village 3 is called the Village of New Beginnings. People who have accepted and grieved their loss can move on to Village 3. At this point they begin to think about making a new life for themselves. They are ready to go out with their friends and have fun again. Those who have lost their spouse may begin to think about another marriage. If they lost a child they may want to have a new baby. But people are changed by the loss; they will not be the same as they were before. If they have grieved well, they might even be stronger people who are able to help others.

D. Not always a direct journey.

It is quite normal for people to revisit previous villages for a short period of time. Someone who has arrived at Village 2 may re-experience a few days of feeling very angry and then leave that behind again. Sometimes people may even start in Village 2 and then go to Village 1 later. Someone may have arrived in Village 3, but move back into the hopelessness of Village 2 in response to some event like the anniversary of a death. This may last for a week or so. All this is normal. Gradually a person moves more and more into the Village of New Beginnings.

What is not good is for someone to stay in Village 1 or 2 for a very long time. For example, a woman may still think she can see or hear her husband a year after he is dead. A mother of a dead child may keep his clothes ready for him, and won't give them away a year or more after the death. A man may still be unwilling to go to social events with his friends two years after his wife has died. These people have stayed in Village 1 or 2 too long, and may need special help to move on.

 **DISCUSSION IN TWOS**

In the loss you mentioned earlier, did you come through all the villages to the

place of new beginnings? Do you feel you got stuck along the way? Did you loop back at all?

4. What Can Make Grieving More Difficult?

Grieving is hard work, but some things can make it even more difficult. These can be things about how the loss happened, or beliefs people have about grief.

A. The type of loss can make grieving more difficult.

Most losses need to be grieved, but these losses are especially difficult:

- When there are too many deaths or losses at the same time.
- When the death or loss is sudden and unexpected.
- When the death or loss is violent.
- When there is no body there to bury.
- When there is no way to confirm that the person has died.
- When the person that provided for the family has died, or the leader of the community.
- When the bereaved have unresolved problems with the dead person.
- When the death is a suicide or murder.
- When a child has died.

B. The false bridge can prevent people from grieving.

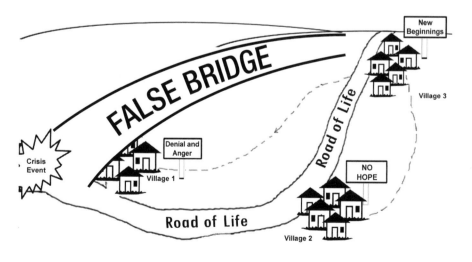

The False Bridge

Some Christians think that since they have the Gospel and all the promises of God, it would be wrong to feel angry or sad about a loss. Some people call this the false bridge, because it appears to provide a straight path from the moment of the loss directly to the "New Beginnings," without passing through Villages 1 and 2. This is not biblical, and it will not bring healing. God made us with the need to grieve our losses. Jesus expressed painful emotions on the cross when he said, "My God, my God, why have you abandoned me?" (Matthew 27:46). He also wept when Lazarus died (John 11:35).

Facing the pain of loss takes courage. We are tempted to avoid it. Sometimes we get busy doing God's work as a way to avoid feeling the pain. This is dangerous, because if we do not grieve a loss when it happens, the grief will stay in us. It will not go away and it can cause problems for many years.

C. Beliefs about crying/weeping can keep us from grieving.

Some cultures require people to cry publicly when someone dies. Those who don't cry are suspected of not caring about the person who died, or of having caused the death. This can result in people crying dramatically, whether they feel sad or not. Other cultures do not allow people, especially men, to cry. This can result in people holding their grief inside rather than letting it out.

Tears are a way God has provided for sadness to leave our body. Weeping can be an important part of grieving, for men as well as women. Even Jesus wept when his close friend Lazarus died (John 11:33-38a). The Psalmist wept (Psalms 6:6; 39:12; 42:1), as did the prophets (Isaiah 22:4; Jeremiah 9:1). Ecclesiastes 3:4 says there is a time to weep. God notices our tears; they are precious to him (Isaiah 38:3-5).

People should not hold their tears inside, nor should they cry just for show. As much as possible, they should let their tears flow naturally. Sometimes the sadness comes at unexpected moments, even months after the loss.

 DISCUSSION IN TWOS

Think again of the loss you experienced. Were there things that prevented you from grieving? What were they? Did your tears help let the pain out?

5. How Can We Help Those Who Are Grieving?

 SMALL GROUP DISCUSSION

1. When you have been mourning someone, what sort of helpful things have people done or said? What sort of unhelpful things have been done or said? Have some groups discuss the first question, and some the second. Then report back to the large group.

2. How does our culture traditionally help those who mourn? What customs are helpful? Which ones are not helpful? Are there any that would not be good for a Christian to do? Why?

A. The example of Job's comforters.

Job was a wealthy man with a large family. In an instant, he lost everything: his children, his cattle, his wealth, his health. When his friends heard about Job's problems, they came to comfort him. They sat in silence with him for a week before speaking. Then Job broke the silence by expressing his pain. His friends were quick to point out his lack of faith (Job 4:3-6), and that his suffering was due to his sins and the sins of his children (Job 4:7-8). Although Job claimed he had not sinned, they were sure that if he were innocent God would not have let this happen (Job 8:6-8; 11:2-4; 22:21-30). They accused him over and over to try to get him to confess. Finally Job says, "You are all miserable comforters!" Rather than comforting Job, they increased his pain.

 DISCUSSION QUESTION

What things did Job's comforters do that were helpful? What things did they do that were not helpful?

B. How can we help people who are grieving?

Some traditional ceremonies and practices help a person grieve. Others do not. Church leaders should encourage those ceremonies which are helpful and are in keeping with the Christian faith. In addition to these things, other ways to help a person grieve are listed here.

- Visit them. Pray for them when they are ready for prayer (Ephesians 6:18).

- When they are ready, encourage them to talk about how they feel. Allow them to express their anger and sadness.

- Listen to their pain. Do more listening than talking. Healing will come as they let the pain out. They cannot absorb teaching and sermons at this time.

- Help them with practical things. If grieving people have to worry about caring for themselves and their families, they will not have energy to mourn properly and recover. They might be too exhausted to do the work they did before, much less to do all the things the deceased person did. Relieve them of their regular responsibilities so that they can grieve. Especially at the time of the funeral and burial, there are many practical ways to help a grieving person. Widows and orphans are in particular need of help, and we are instructed to care for them: "What God the Father considers to be pure and genuine religion is this: to take care of orphans and widows in their suffering and to keep oneself from being corrupted by the world (James 1:27).

- Help them to understand that it is normal to grieve, and that it is a process that will take time. They will not always feel like they do today. It is important that they do not make major changes, like marrying someone, based on how they feel as they go through Villages 1 and 2. When they are in Village 3, they will be able to make better decisions.

- If there is no body, arrange a church service to remember the person's life and to publicly acknowledge his or her death. A photo of the person or a cross can take the place of the missing loved one. If the family is dispersed, those who are displaced can hold similar ceremonies.

- It is not unusual for a person to have difficulty sleeping in the early weeks and months after a loss. If people are not able to sleep, encourage them to do some hard work, to take walks, or to get involved in sports. Getting exhausted will help them sleep better at night.

- If the person denies that their loved one has died, gently help them realize it in small ways. For example, help the person to disperse of the loved one's personal belongings.

- When people are ready, you can read them a promise from God's Word, and encourage them to memorize it, for example Psalms 34:18, Isaiah 63:9, or John 14:1.

- Eventually, they need to bring their pain to God. The more specific they can be about their loss, the better. For example, they may not only have lost a loved one, but also an income, companionship, respect, or security. They should bring these losses to the Lord one by one.

# CLOSING EXERCISE

1. *Divide into small groups. Using what you have learned, make up skits of a pastor visiting someone who has just lost his or her spouse. The skits should first show the wrong way to listen and then, in a second scene, the right way. Present the skits to the large group.*

2. *Art exercise: Have markers and paper or modeling clay available. Have everyone get quiet inside and ask God to show them the pain in their hearts. Now begin drawing or modeling clay without thinking about it, letting the pain come out through their fingers. Drawings may be symbolic rather than realistic. For example, churches may be represented by circles, or the dead by crosses. Each person will use symbols that mean something to him or her. For example, a cigarette may represent a brother who smokes. Colors can be used to represent feelings or objects too. For example, black and red could symbolize the earthquake and yellow could be the help that arrived. Allow 30-45 minutes for people to work individually. Then in small groups discuss what they have done and what it might mean.*

Lesson 4

HOW CAN WE HELP CHILDREN WHO HAVE EXPERIENCED BAD THINGS?

1. The Story of Lilienne

Lilienne was always a happy child. With four brothers and sisters in a modest home, this seven-year-old never had a lot of clothes or toys, but she loved the simple things of life. Her parents would hear her singing softly in the middle of the night. Her teachers would see her dancing in the playground, just twirling with joy. She especially enjoyed the Christian songs she learned at school.

She was at home with her mother when the ground shook. All her brothers and sisters were out playing, but Lilienne was helping to fix dinner. She remembers being across the room from her mother, but unable to run to her. Terrified, she froze in place for 40 seconds as the walls leaned back and forth and furniture fell over, A piece of the roof fell a foot in front of her. She could not breathe. Suddenly her mother was there, scooping her up and carrying her outside. Over her mother's shoulder, she looked back to see the house fall in upon itself.

Life changed for the whole family. They had to live in the park with many others, stretching bedsheets on poles to provide shade and a little privacy. One of her brothers was missing for about a week, but eventually found. Her father had worked at a store, but that building was destroyed in the quake, so he was without a job. Though he had made it through the earthquake with only minor bruises, he got knocked in the head while fighting to get food for the family. He had to sleep for several days.

At Lilienne's school, one of the buildings had fallen, but the other remained standing, and so the children crowded into the classrooms there. Although she had always loved school, now Lilienne didn't want to go. It was hard to pay attention to the teacher. Lilienne kept looking up at the ceiling, wondering when it would fall. Her teacher was upset because she didn't do her homework. Even worse, she didn't dance in the playground anymore.

And she didn't sing at night. Instead, as the family settled down in their tent city, with moans and snores all around them, Lilienne would toss and turn and often wake up crying. Her parents don't know what to do.

 DISCUSSION QUESTIONS

> *1. How did Lilienne behave before, during, and after the earthquake?*
>
> *2. Why do you think her behavior changed after the earthquake?*
>
> *3. How do adults usually react to children like Lilienne? Do you think these reactions are helpful?*

2. How Do Children Who Have Experienced Scary or Horrible and Confusing Things Behave?

When children experience bad things, they are affected in many ways.

A. Their emotions are affected.

- They may become fearful. Small children might cling to their parents. They may be afraid of strangers or of the dark. They may jump or cry when they hear loud noises. They may be afraid something horrible will happen again. They may be afraid to go to school.

- They may become angry and aggressive. Small children may fight with their playmates more than before. Older children may rebel against their parents and teachers more than before.

- They may become sad. Even though a child is very sad, such as after someone dies, it is normal for him to stay sad for a while, and then play for a while.

- They may lose interest in life. The pain in their hearts preoccupies their minds. It saps their energy for life.
- Older children may feel guilty that they survived and others did not. Even adults can feel this way. They may be afraid that something they said or did is the reason someone else died—even though this is not true.

B. Their bodies are affected.

- Their speech may be affected. They may begin to stutter, or they may become mute.
- They may lose their appetite because they are anxious, or they may eat too much to try to kill the pain.
- They may complain of headaches, stomach aches, or other aches in their bodies. They may have hives or asthma.

C. Their behavior is affected.

- They may go back to behaving like they did when they were younger. For example, children can start wetting the bed or sucking their thumbs again.
- They may have nightmares and bad dreams. Some small children may scream in their sleep without even being awake. This usually stops as they grow older.
- They may play fight with playmates.
- They may fight a lot and be irritable.
- They may cry a lot.
- They may be especially upset if they lose things that matter to them, like clothes or a toy or a book.
- They may do poorly at school because they can't concentrate.
- Older children may drink alcohol or take drugs to kill their pain, or become involved in wrong sexual relations.
- Older children may take risks, like riding fast on a motorcycle or running away from home. This makes them feel brave in the face of danger.
- Older children may hurt themselves, for example cutting their bodies or committing suicide.

 DISCUSSION QUESTION

Do you know any children who have experienced scary and horrible things? How do they behave?

3. How Do We Help Children Like Lilienne?

A. Parents need to reunite the family, if possible, and re-establish routines or create new routines.

It is important that families be brought together quickly after the bad event, if that is possible.

The more predictable each day's activities are, the better for the children. Each day Lilienne should know what is likely to happen. She should be encouraged to go to school, help her mother, and play with his friends. Part of the activities should be having fun together. This may be playing games or telling folk tales. It is important to try to finish activities that have been started. This gives the child the sense that she or he is able to accomplish something. It restores the child's sense of security. It helps the child feel that the future is not out of control.

If there is tension between the father and mother, the children will sense it, and become more afraid. They may even think it is their fault for their parents' tension. Parents need to resolve any tensions there might be between them, for their own sakes and for the sakes of their children.

B. Parents need to listen to their children's pain.

Children know more about what is going on around them than adults realize. They tend to fill in missing information in whatever way makes sense to them. If they do not have a chance to talk about things, they may get very wrong, strange ideas in their heads. Even if parents are not used to talking with their children, it is very important that they do so when terrible things are going on, as well as afterwards. This is not the time to say, "Go away and play." Families should talk together about the awful things that happened. Children should have the chance to say what they felt when the terrible things happened. It is quite possible that some of the other children who are not showing that they have problems in fact do, and they should have the chance to share these. It is also good for parents to talk with each child individually.

Younger children are often better able to express things through play than by talking. When children play earthquake, it helps them work out the pain they experienced. Parents should ask them about what they are playing and how they feel about it. Then they can go from talking about the play earthquake to talking about the child's real experience that he is suffering from.

Another way to help children talk about their pain is through drawing. Parents can give them paper and pencils, or if these are not available, have them draw in the sand. If they don't know what to draw, ask them to draw a man, then their family, then where they used to live. Ask them to explain their drawing to you. Remember that the goal is to help them talk about their pain, not to teach them.

If children have bad dreams, explain that many times people dream about terrible things that have happened to them. Encourage them to talk about their dreams. Ask them if they think their dream could be related to something that happened to them.

 SMALL GROUP DISCUSSION

1. *How can a way be provided for children to talk about their painful experiences?*

2. *Traditionally, do parents talk to their children in your area?*

3. *If they do not, what beliefs keep them from doing so?*

4. *How do these beliefs compare with Scripture? (Read the following passages.)*

Mark 10:13-16: People were bringing little children to Jesus to have him touch them, but the disciples rebuked them. When Jesus saw this, he was indignant. He said to them, "Let the little children come to me, and do not hinder them, for the kingdom of God belongs to such as these. I tell you the truth, anyone who will not receive the kingdom of God like a little child will never enter it." And he took the children in his arms, put his hands on them and blessed them.

Deuteronomy 6:4-9: Hear, O Israel: The Lord our God, the Lord is one. Love the Lord your God with all your heart and with all your soul and with all your strength. These commandments that I give you today are to be upon your hearts. Impress them on your children. Talk about them when you sit at home and when you walk along the road, when you lie down and when you get up. Tie them as symbols on your hands and bind them on your foreheads. Write them on the doorframes of your houses and on your gates.

C. Parents need to tell children the truth about the situation.

Children need to understand the truth of what has happened, in ways appropriate for their age. They should be told whether or not there is still danger and whether or not someone has died. Knowing the real danger is better than imagining all sorts of dangers that are not true. At the same time, parents should not exaggerate the danger or speak of all the terrible things that could possibly happen.

Parents should make a plan for what they will do if something else awful happens, and discuss this openly with the family.

D. Parents need to have family devotions daily.

A good time to talk together as a family is at the end of the day. Each person, young and old, should talk about what he or she has seen or felt that day. Small children also need a chance to talk and to give their prayer requests. Then the family should all pray and sing together. Remember, as soon as children can talk to other people, they can talk to God. Terrible things can bring a family closer together if they are handled in the right way.

Often small children do not understand death. They expect the person to come back. They ask questions like: Why did God let this happen? Will he let it happen to me? Was it my fault? What will happen to the body after it's buried? If I got to sleep will I wake up? Some of their questions may be difficult to answer completely, but parents should answer as best they can and in ways that encourage the child to trust God.

Each family member needs to be helped to know that God is still there and cares for him or her. Each person could choose a verse to memorize, for example:

- God is a watchman that never sleeps (Psalms 121:4).

- God can take all our fears (1 Peter 5:7).

- God is like a person who takes good care of animals (Psalms 23).

- God is always there as our refuge or shelter (Psalms 46:1).

- God wants us to trust him (Proverbs 3:5).

- God is gentle and patient (Matthew 11:29).

E. Teenagers have particular needs.

Children between the ages of 12 and 20 are going through a difficult period of life even when there are no disasters. Some problems that may arise after a traumatic situation may be due simply to the age of the child.

Teenagers have a need for their own private space. This is particularly true for teenage girls. This may be difficult when families are displaced from their homes, but understanding a teenage girl's need for privacy can help, even if parents are not able to provide her very much of it.

Teenagers have a need to discuss things with their peers, and this should be encouraged. Sometimes teenage girls are kept so busy in the home that they do not have a chance to talk with their friends. After a traumatic event, they need this chance to talk even more than normally.

Teenagers need to feel useful especially when their family is going through difficulties. If they can do things that help their family or others survive, this will give them a sense of worth.

F. Parents need to help teachers and school administrators understand what is happening.

Parents and other leaders should arrange a time to meet with the school director and teachers to discuss what has happened.

They need to understand how the trouble has affected the children and their performance at school. If the teachers understand the situation, they will be more patient with the students, and will be a part of the healing process.

G. Serious cases.

If after a year there is a child who is still showing serious problems, some mature, wise person needs to spend a lot of time with that child. God can heal the child, but it will take time. He or she may need professional help.

# CLOSING SMALL GROUP EXERCISE

Read Deuteronomy 6:4-9 or Matthew 18:1-6 together.

Deuteronomy 6:4-9: Hear, O Israel: The Lord our God, the Lord is one. Love the Lord your God with all your heart and with all your soul and with all your strength. These commandments that I give you today are to be upon your hearts. Impress them on your children. Talk about them when you sit at home and when you walk along the road, when you lie down and when you get up. Tie them as symbols on your hands and bind them on your foreheads. Write them on the doorframes of your houses and on your gates.

Matthew 18:1-6: At that time the disciples came to Jesus and asked, "Who is the greatest in the kingdom of heaven?" He called a little child and had him stand among them. And he said: "I tell you the truth, unless you change and become like little children, you will never enter the kingdom of heaven. Therefore, whoever humbles himself like this child is the greatest in the kingdom of heaven. And whoever welcomes a little child like this in my name welcomes me. But if anyone causes one of these little ones who believes in me to sin, it would be better for him to have a large millstone hung around his neck and to be drowned in the depths of the sea.

- *Discuss how the passage challenges us in how we treat our children.*
- *Discuss what children in your area need special help and plan what can be done for them.*
- *Then pray together for these children.*

Lesson 5

HOW CAN WE HELP WOMEN WHO HAVE BEEN RAPED?

1. The Story of Anna

Chaos reigned on the streets of the city. So many people had lost their homes that every open space became a tent city, with sheets strung along to provide some small sense of privacy. Still, screams and sobs could be heard throughout the night, every night. So no one paid much attention to Anna's cries for help.

She had been on the outskirts of town that day, searching for food and water for her husband and parents. Someone said the military was dropping supplies in that area, so she hurried out there. It was a long day of waiting and struggling with others, but she managed to get a few bottles and some grains and plantains. The trip back was difficult, with disturbances on some streets and other streets torn up by the earthquake. Then darkness was falling, and she had a hard time finding her way with so many of the old landmarks in ruins. She was just a block away from the tent city when she was grabbed from behind. Her supplies clattered to the ground as a violent man tore her clothing. She called and called for her husband, hoping he might hear through the dense night, but he did not hear her so he could not rescue her. She was raped.

Anna gathered up the food and water and returned to the tent. She felt ashamed, too ashamed to tell her family. She sewed her clothing the next day and made up a story about her bruises. A week later she finally told her husband. He said comforting words to her, but he was also very angry and confused. He knew in his head that the rape was not Anna's fault, but because of what had happened, he didn't want to touch her anymore.

In the following weeks, Anna felt so sad and awful that she thought about killing herself. Then she thought she might be pregnant, and this confused her even more. In great anguish, she went to talk to the pastor's wife.

It felt good to talk about it, even though Anna cried through most of the conversation. The pastor's wife was a good listener. She asked Anna's permission to tell her husband, the pastor, about this, so he could help Anna's husband. Anna agreed.

And so the healing process began, with the pastor and his wife encouraging Anna and her husband to talk about their true feelings. A terrible thing had happened to both of them, and they both needed to express their pain. If they kept their feelings hidden, the pastor explained, they would become a wall between them. They needed to open their hearts fully in love.

 DISCUSSION QUESTIONS

1. Why didn't Anna tell anyone immediately what happened to her?

2. What was her husband's problem?

3. How did they both find healing?

2. What Is Rape?

Rape is when a person forces themselves sexually on another person without their consent. Most often, it is a man forcing himself on a woman or girl, but it can also happen to a boy or man. Even during normal times, rape is a problem, but in times of chaos, it is far more frequent. Rape can be an act of lust , but most often it is an act of violence and provides a false sense of power for the rapist. Rape may be committed by a family member, a trusted friend, or a total stranger.

3. What Are the Effects of Rape?

 DISCUSSION QUESTIONS

1. Do you know of anyone who has been raped? How do you think the rape affected her or him? The family?

2. Do you know anyone who has raped a woman? How has it affected him?

Rape is one of the most painful experiences a woman can go through. It leaves deep wounds in her heart which last for a long time. Because women feel ashamed by rape, the wounds it causes are often kept very secret. No one else ever knows what happened. Just because a woman does not talk about being raped does not mean it hasn't happened to her.

The fears and feelings in a female who has been raped are much the same for a boy who has been raped. He may feel emasculated and may fear never having a normal male/female relationship, or he may try to have many female sexual conquests in order to prove his masculinity. Conversely, he may either be afraid he is a homosexual or may want to think he is.

A. How does rape affect a person?

Women are usually victims of rape and so the female pronoun is used below. But be aware that a raped boy may feel many of the same things.

- She will feel a deep sense of shame. She may feel covered with a dirtiness she cannot remove.

- She may feel ruined, that she no longer has any value. If she is not married, she may feel that no one will ever want to marry her. She may be very sad to the point of wanting to kill herself.

- She may be angry at all men. She may be angry at God for letting it happen. This anger may be let out on anyone who is with her.

- She may feel guilty and think God is punishing her. She may ask, "What did I do to cause this to happen to me?" Others may reinforce this feeling by accusing her of being responsible for the rape.

- She may be afraid to tell anyone. If they knew, they might accuse her of lying or blame her for what happened. Her husband or suitors might reject her, and the community may look down on her.

- She may no longer be able to enjoy sexual relations, and even become frigid (stiff with fear about sex). Or she may begin having sex with lots of men, because she feels that she is ruined and worthless.

- She may have injured sexual organs or other internal organs. As a woman struggles against the rapist, she may break bones or get other injuries. She could get AIDS, or other sexually transmitted diseases, or become pregnant. She might want to abort the baby. These things could lead to sterility.

- She may be unable to trust God to protect her in the future.

- She may think demons have possessed her.

B. How does rape affect the woman's marriage and family?

If the rape was done by a stranger, the family and community may be compassionate towards the woman. If they witnessed the rape and were unable or afraid to stop it, they may feel as violated as the girl herself, or feel guilt that they didn't stop it.

If the woman does not tell her family, they will not be able to understand why she is sad and angry. Her husband may not understand why having sex is so difficult for her now.

If she tells her family about it, and the rape was done by someone they know, they might not want to admit that the father, uncle, brother, or pastor has done this bad thing. They may be afraid to accuse the rapist, especially if he is a respected member of the family or community. To keep the peace, they may deny that it happened and tell the girl she's lying. Or, if they believe that it happened, they might blame the girl for flirting with the rapist, and they may punish her. Or they may plan how to take revenge. In any case, rape will cause serious problems in the woman's marriage and family.

The woman's husband is especially affected by the rape. He may feel his wife is now polluted, and he may no longer want to be with her. When this happens, it adds to her feelings of shame and isolation.

C. How does rape affect the rapist?

Often rapists seem proud of what they have done, but the violence they do to others also kills something inside them.

If the man is a Christian, he may feel very guilty and ashamed. He will be even more afraid than the woman to tell others about what he did. He will be a man full of internal struggles. His shame may be so great that it leads him to kill himself.

4. How Can We Help Someone Who Has Been Raped?

A. She needs medical care.

The rape victim needs immediate medical care, if possible. There are medicines which can be given immediately after a rape which make it less likely that the woman will contract HIV, sexually transmitted diseases, tetanus, hepatitis B, or other illnesses. A doctor should check her for other infections and injuries, for example, broken bones or internal bleeding.

It is better if the person gets medical help within one or two days after the rape. Even if there is a delay, getting help within two weeks is still worthwhile. Somebody should go with the person to the doctor and stay with her there. This comforts and supports the person, and may help her give the necessary information to the doctor. This can be a member of the family, a friend or an older, caring woman, if the victim is a woman.

 SMALL GROUP DISCUSSION

What resources are available in your area to provide medical help to rape victims? If you don't know, make a plan to find out.

B. She needs to have a person to talk to who she can trust.

Since rape makes a woman feel so deeply ashamed, she will only share her pain with someone she trusts in order to keep the matter private. Since rape victims already feel bad about themselves, they will not want to share their pain with people who reprimand or blame them more for what happened. Often the woman knows whom she can trust, and she should be allowed to choose whom she talks to. It could be a pastor, a pastor's wife, a wise woman in the church, or another woman who has been raped. Pastors can identify people in the church who are able to do this, and give them training to improve their skills.

When a woman talks to someone about her rape experience, it is very personal and a bond can form between them. Because of this, it is better if a woman talks with the raped woman. If a man is talking with her, it would be better that another woman be present. This could be either the man's wife or a mature woman in the church. If another woman cannot be present, his wife and someone else in the church should know that he is talking with the raped woman, and when and where this is taking place.

Some women will not feel free to share their pain with anyone. For this reason, pastors should include prayers and teaching for rape victims in their services. This might bring a ray of hope to someone who has deep, secret pain. It may also help her realize that she can talk about this subject with others.

The counselor must enable the victim to talk openly about what has happened and what she is feeling. She should be allowed to say how angry and ashamed she feels. It is very common for rape victims to be angry at God. This is okay. God is able to accept her anger and still love her. It is better for her to be truthful about feelings than to hide them. Writing a lament would be a good way to get the feelings out (See Lesson 2, Section 3).

The first step in healing is when the woman realizes the impact of the rape on her life. This comes about by her talking about it and someone listening to her attentively and understanding how she is feeling. She will need a lot of time to talk about this over the following days and months.

 DISCUSSION IN TWOS

1. If you had a big problem, who would you talk to?

2. What sort of people in your church could be trained to help raped women?

C. She needs to know that she is loved.

At first, the woman may be so angry at God that she is not willing to pray or listen to God's Word. The only love she might be able to accept is that of those around her. By seeing that others still value and love her, she will gradually realize that she is not ruined. Her husband and family members can play a key role in this. Eventually, she may be willing to receive comfort from God's Word and have others pray for her. Some Scriptures that might be helpful are Psalms 9:9-10; 10:17-18.

Psalms 9:9-10: The Lord is a refuge for the oppressed, a stronghold in times of trouble. Those who know your name will trust in you for you, Lord, have never forsaken those who seek you.

Psalms 10:17-18: You hear, O Lord, the desire of the afflicted; you encourage them, and you listen to their cry, defending the fatherless and the oppressed, in order that man, who is of the earth, may terrify no more.

D. She needs to bring her pain to God.

When she is ready, she needs to bring her pain to God in prayer and ask him to heal her. The more specific she can be about what she lost in the rape—for example, her innocence, her purity, her joy—the better. She should ask God to restore these things to her (Psalms 71:20).

E. She needs to eventually forgive the person who raped her.

When the pain in her heart has been healed by God, then she can begin to forgive the rapist. He did a terrible thing, but God asks us to forgive those who do evil to us (Matthew 6:14-15). The process of forgiveness may take a long time. If a child resulted from the rape, forgiving the rapist in her heart will help her more fully accept the child.

5. What about Children Born Out of Rape?

A. What are their special needs?

Sometimes, children born out of rape are rejected by their mothers and families. They may be treated poorly, or even neglected so much that they die. They may be ridiculed for not having a father. Their siblings may hate them and not consider them to be full members of the family.

B. How can we help these children?

God has a special love for the fatherless (Deuteronomy 10:18). In Psalms 68:5-6, it says: "God, who lives in his sacred Temple, cares for orphans and protects widows. He gives the lonely a home to live in and leads prisoners out into happy freedom, but rebels will have to live in a desolate land." As Christians, we should ask God to give us his special love for these children. They are not responsible for the bad things that have been done to them. They need our love even more than other children. They need special teaching from God's Word to assure them that their life is not an accident. Some Scriptures that might be helpful are Psalms 139:14-18, Isaiah 49:15, and 1 Corinthians 1:27-29.

When they begin asking who their father is, it is good to tell them the truth. They most likely know more than people think they know. If the father is known, let them know who it is. If he is already dead at that time, it may be helpful to tell them who the relatives are.

The pastor will need to help the whole family to accept a child like this. The husband may find this difficult, and even older brothers and sisters may struggle with it. When the time comes for the baby to be dedicated or baptized in church, this is a good time to ask for a special blessing on the baby and the family.

 DISCUSSION QUESTION

Are there any children in your church who are teased or despised because of the events surrounding their birth? If so, how are you helping them?

6. How Can We Help the Rapist?

Rapists need to know that Jesus will forgive their sin (Isaiah 1:18). They may have raped more than once. They may continue to have a burning desire to have sex with women and think they can't overcome it. They need to have someone to whom they can confess their sin. This person needs to pray with them and keep them accountable for their actions day by day so that they will never do it again.

The rapist needs to take full responsibility for what he has done. He needs to ask his victim(s) to forgive him. Although he can never restore a woman's purity, he should do whatever he can to help her as a visible sign of his repentance. There may be legal consequences he will have to face.

If the church knows that a member raped someone, the pastor should talk to him about it. If he confesses and repents, the church should extend the same forgiveness God has given to the rapist. If he does not repent, he should be excluded from the church, both to protect other women from him and to bring him to repentance.

# CLOSING SMALL GROUP EXERCISE

Imagine that Anna is a member of your church. She has told the pastor what has happened. How do you think your church would help Anna? Be realistic!

HOW CAN A CHURCH MINISTER IN THE MIDST OF HIV/AIDS?

It would be helpful to have an informed medical person present during this session.

1. The Story of Emile and Yvette

Emile was a farmer in the northern part of the country. He was happily married to Yvette and they had four children. Since they were both committed Christians, they knew it is wrong to sleep with anyone but your wife or husband. They'd heard about AIDS, but didn't really understand how you catch it. Years ago, Emile was asked to take a course at the university on better farming methods. Emile was proud to be selected for this class. He was excited as he boarded the colorful tap-tap bus that took him to the capital city for the four-month course.

The course was hard at first and Emile spent all his time studying. (He had never been a very good reader.) But by the second month, he was doing better. He even had some free time. Some other men in the class invited him to go out with them at night. At first he refused. He wasn't sure what kind of trouble they would get into. But finally he said yes.

The city was full of temptations. Emile was dazzled by the music and dancing, the bamboche festivals, the bars and the women, Women he didn't know would flirt openly with him on the street. By this time Emile was missing his wife very much. He spent a lot of time each day thinking about her—and about women in general. Now at the bar, his new friends were urging him to sleep with a prostitute. They said he wasn't a "real man" if he didn't. The teasing, the temptation, and his loneliness grew too much for him. He gave in.

The next day he felt awful about what he had done with the prostitute. He confessed his sin to God and resolved never to do this again. At the end of the course Emile happily returned to his family.

Two more years passed and now they had five children with a sixth on the way. When he began to feel unwell, he had almost forgotten about sleeping with the prostitute. At first he was just generally tired and started losing weight. Then he started having strange rashes and also frequent diarrhea. After a while he went to the doctor. The doctor examined him and gave him various blood tests. Finally the doctor called him into his office and broke the sad news that he was HIV positive. He told him that he might already have infected his wife and even the unborn child.

Yvette went to the hospital for the HIV test and found out that, indeed, she was HIV positive. They told her that if she took some special medicine during the rest of her pregnancy, the baby was less likely to be born HIV positive. So she faithfully went to the hospital for these medicines and the baby was born healthy—but then Yvette began to feel sick herself. Both she and Emile were in despair as they thought of the future of their six children. They were afraid to tell anyone of their problem in case people would start to avoid them. But soon the problem was too big for them to bear alone, and they told their pastor.

 DISCUSSION QUESTIONS

1. In your area, do people tell others if they know they have HIV or AIDS? Why or why not?

2. If they do not tell, how do you know when someone has AIDS?

3. How do people in your community treat people with HIV or AIDS?

2. What Do You Know about HIV/AIDS?

Try this quiz. The answers are at the end of the chapter.

1. What does AIDS stand for?

2. What does HIV stand for?

3. What is the most frequent way that people worldwide are infected with HIV?

4. What is the second most frequent way?

5. Is there a cure for AIDS?

6. Is it possible for you to be infected by HIV by doing the following? Mark each one yes or no.

    a. Shaking hands with someone infected by HIV.

    b. Receiving an injection.

    c. Sharing food from the same bowl with someone with HIV.

    d. Using the same toilet as someone who has HIV.

    e. Using a razor blade that has been already used by another person.

    f. Having sex with someone who has HIV.

    g. Hugging a person with AIDS.

    h. Washing the sores of a person with AIDS without gloves.

7. Can you tell by looking that someone has HIV?

8. What is the only way to tell for sure if you have HIV?

3. What Are Some Beliefs That Increase the Spread of AIDS?

Some people believe things that are not true about sex and AIDS. These lies keep them from protecting themselves from AIDS. Here are some of them:

- *A man who does not have sex for some time will go mad or become impotent. Or young people need sex to develop normally. Or having sex will help a man get over an illness.* These things are not true. Men do not need to have sex to develop normally, recover from illness, be sane, or remain fertile. Remember, Jesus was celibate.

- *A woman should prove she is fertile before marriage.* This is not true. In the Bible, all sexual relations outside marriage are considered sexual immorality, and sexual immorality is sin (Galatians 5:19). Children are a blessing, but they are not necessary for a Christian marriage (Genesis 2:18).

- *If Satan tempts you to sexual sin, you can't resist.* This is not true. The Bible says, "Resist the Devil and he will flee from you" (James 4:7). God will always give you a way to escape temptation. 1 Corinthians 10:13 says, "Every test that you have experienced is the kind that normally comes to people. But God keeps his promise, and he will not allow you to be tested beyond your power to remain firm; at the time you are put to the test, he will give you the strength to endure it, and so provide you with a way out."

- *AIDS is a curse from God or it is caused by spirits.* AIDS is directly linked to people's behavior. There is no mystery about how a person contracts it.

- *A person who tells you that you have HIV/AIDS is cursing you, so it is better not to say anything.* This is not true either, and when people do keep quiet about HIV/AIDS, it allows them to go on infecting others, who unknowingly infect others. We should react to the threat of AIDS as we would react to the threat of a wild animal roaming the streets. Cry out! Let people know about the danger!

 DISCUSSION QUESTION

What are some other things that people believe in your area about the spread of AIDS? Get someone who is medically trained, such as a doctor or dispensary nurse, to help you and your people know if these things are true.

4. What Are Some Practices that Increase the Spread of AIDS?

Some cultures have customs or rituals that favor the spread of AIDS. Here are some:

- Levirate marriage (for example, a man may be obliged to marry the widow of his dead brother). If the dead brother died of AIDS, the widow will possibly bring AIDS into her new family.

- Polygamy or placage, in which a man is allowed to keep multiple wives or mistresses.

- The low status of women which denies them the freedom to make choices about their sexuality and reproductive health.

- Funeral practices that involve contact with the body fluids of the dead person.

- Religious or occult rituals that involve the shedding, sharing, or drinking of blood.

- Sharing needles for injections with others.

- Circumcision.

 DISCUSSION QUESTIONS

1. Are there practices in your area that increase the spread of AIDS?

2. What are they?

3. What can we do about these things?

5. How Can We Teach Children about Sex and AIDS?

 DISCUSSION QUESTION

How do children learn about sex? Who teaches them? At what age does this take place?

The most likely way a young person will get infected with HIV is through sexual activity. The church needs to help those who teach children about sex know the facts about AIDS. Sex and AIDS education needs to start by the age of ten, or earlier if they ask questions. This education should be given before they become sexually active. Some very good books are available to teach children about sex and about AIDS. These could be translated into your language.

Having many sexual partners increases the chances of getting AIDS and is displeasing to God. Non-Christian agencies promote the use of condoms as a way to avoid contracting AIDS. Condoms reduce the probability of getting AIDS, but abstinence before marriage is the only completely safe way to avoid getting AIDS. It also follows the Biblical teaching of reserving sex for marriage. (The Bible also warns against incest [1 Corinthians 5:1]).This teaching may challenge the dominant sexual practices of your culture. Young people will need a lot of encouragement to remain pure in this area. The example of the adults will speak louder than any teaching that is given.

Youth have a lot of energy. They need to be involved in good activities. If the church involves them in caring for people with AIDS, there can be many benefits.

- It makes them feel wanted and needed by the church.

- It helps them see the dangers of getting HIV/AIDS.

- It gives them something good to do so that they are not so likely to do bad things.

Youth can develop ways to teach AIDS awareness to others, through drama, song, presentations, or Bible study. They can visit the sick and read Scripture to them. They can do practical things to help them, like bringing water or food.

1. Are there any activities in your church that are useful and enjoyable for young people (ages 10-20)?

2. What can your church do to help parents (or other appropriate people) teach young people about AIDS and sex?

3. How could young people in your church be involved in helping others avoid AIDS or in ministering to those who have it?

6. How Can the Church Help a Person with HIV/AIDS?

Churches need to train a group of helpers to minister to those with AIDS (Matthew 25: 34-36). Often these helpers go out two by two. AIDS victims need help in all areas of their lives.

A. Tell them about Jesus and the Bible.

Helpers should read Scripture, pray and sing with the sick person and his family. If the sick person is a Christian, he will receive much comfort from hearing about heaven. If the sick person is not a Christian, often he is open to hearing about how his sins can be forgiven, and how he can be sure he is going to heaven.

As the sick person begins to trust the helper, he can tell them how he is feeling about life and his illness. It is also important that the sick person knows he can tell God exactly how he feels. Psalms 38, where David expresses his real feelings to God when he was sick, might provide a model for AIDS victims. AIDS victims may want to use this as a model for their own laments (See Lesson 2, Section 3b).

> **Psalms 38:** O Lord, do not rebuke me in your anger or discipline me in your wrath. For your arrows have pierced me, and your hand has come down upon me. Because of your wrath there is no health in my body; my bones have no soundness because of my sin. My guilt has overwhelmed me like a burden too heavy to bear. My wounds fester and are loathsome because of my sinful folly. I am bowed down and brought very low; all the day long I go about mourning. My back is filled with searing pain; there is no health in my body I am feeble and utterly crushed; I groan in anguish of heart. All my longings lie open before you, O Lord; my sighing is not hidden from you. My heart pounds, my strength fails me; even the light has gone from my eyes. My friends and companions avoid me because of my wounds; my neighbors stay far away.

B. Help them tell others about their illness.

Often people want to hide that they are HIV positive. This does not help the sick person or the community as a whole. If they do not tell the real reason they are sick, people may wrongly accuse others of having caused the illness through a curse or witchcraft. It takes a brave person to be the first to say publicly that he or she has AIDS, but this can help others to do so. It is a very necessary step in helping the community avoid the threat of that "wild beast."

Ministering to AIDS Victims

Everyone needs to know how AIDS is spread. It is equally important that they also know they will not catch AIDS by touching a sick person, or eating with them, or taking care of their needs.

C. They should not be excluded from their families or friends.

People need other people! AIDS victims may be rejected by their friends and even their family. The church needs to work with the community to help them accept these sick people and not be scared of them. Those who are suffering from AIDS can help each other by meeting together and sharing their experiences. The church could help to arrange this.

D. Help them understand the grief process.

It comes as a tremendous shock to someone to know that he or she going to die. When someone has a fatal disease, the person often goes through stages that are similar to those that happen when we grieve: anger and denial, depression, and then acceptance. People who help these sick people need to know that it is normal to be angry at first. They may also deny that they have AIDS. A state of depression is also normal, and it may be some months before they can accept they are going to die. They may bargain with God, promising certain behaviors in exchange for their health. A good helper will be patient with them as they go through these stages.

E. Care for their bodies.

Two people may become HIV positive. One may live for six years, another may live for six months. This is partly due to the overall physical well-being of the person, but it is also due to his attitude, and the care he receives. People who have something to do will live longer than those who do nothing, so it is good to give AIDS victims some activity to help the family. They could learn to sew clothes or raise animals or engage in another activity that does not require great physical strength. In addition, good regular food will help the person to fight off disease. It is particularly important that the sick person eats plenty of fruit and vegetables so that they get good vitamins to keep their bodies healthy. They will need a lot of rest, and they should not smoke, or drink much alcohol. In some places, anti-viral drugs may be available that will help. If so, people need to follow the doctor's instructions exactly about taking them. If not they will do more harm than good.

The church also needs to arrange care of orphans whose parents have died of AIDS, and help widows and widowers who may themselves be HIV positive (James 1:27). The church should also help prostitutes find other ways to make a living.

✗ CLOSING EXERCISE

1. *Do you have trained people to visit the sick, or is the pastor expected to do this alone?*

2. *Are all of the five areas listed above covered when you visit the sick? If not, how can you change this?*

3. *Study 1 Corinthians 6:13b-20. Why should a Christian flee from sexual immorality?*

   1 Corinthians 6:13b-20 The body is not meant for sexual immorality, but for the Lord, and the Lord for the body. By his power God raised the Lord from the dead, and he will raise us also. Do you not know that your bodies are members of Christ himself? Shall I then take the members of Christ and unite them with a prostitute? Never! Do you not know that he who unites himself with a prostitute is one with her in body? For it is said, 'The two will become one flesh.' But he who unites himself with the Lord is one with him in spirit. Flee from sexual immorality. All other sins a man commits are outside his body, but he who sins sexually sins against his own body. Do you not know that your body is a temple of the Holy Spirit, who is in you, whom you have received from God? You are not your own; you were bought with a price. Therefore honor God with your body.

4. *Read the following verses. What do they teach about visiting the sick?*

2 Corinthians 1:3-5: Praise be to the God and Father of our Lord Jesus Christ, the Father of compassion and the God of all comfort, who comforts us in all our troubles, so that we can comfort those in any trouble with the comfort we ourselves have received from God. For just as the sufferings of Christ flow over into our lives, so also through Christ our comfort overflows.

1 Corinthians 13:3-8: If I give all I possess to the poor and surrender my body to the flames, but have not love, I gain nothing. Love is patient, love is kind. It does not envy, it does not boast, it is not proud. It is not rude, it is not self-seeking, it is not easily angered, it keeps no record of wrongs. Love does not delight in evil but rejoices with the truth. It always protects, always trusts, always hopes, always perseveres. Love never fails. But where there are prophecies, they will cease; where there are tongues, they will be stilled; where there is knowledge, it will pass away.

2 Corinthians 5:19-20: God was reconciling the world to himself in Christ, not counting men's sins against them. And he has committed to us the message of reconciliation. We are therefore Christ's ambassadors, as though God were making his appeal through us. We implore you on Christ's behalf: Be reconciled to God.

Matthew 25:35-40: For I was hungry and you gave me something to eat, I was thirsty and you gave me something to drink, I was a stranger and you invited me in, I needed clothes and you clothed me, I was sick and you looked after me, I was in prison and you came to visit me. Then the righteous will answer him, "Lord, when did we see you hungry and feed you, or thirsty and give you something to drink? When did we see you a stranger and invite you in, or needing clothes and clothe you? When did we see you sick or in prison and go to visit you?" The King will reply, "I tell you the truth, whatever you did for one of the least of these brothers of mine, you did for me."

5. *What is the one thing you would like to start doing in your church after reading this lesson?*

Answers to the Quiz (PGS. 60-61)

1. Acquired Immune Deficiency Syndrome

2. Human Immunodeficiency Virus

3. Through unprotected sex

4. By mother to child transmission

5. No

6. a. No, b. Yes, c. No, d. No, e. Yes, f. Yes, g. No, h. Yes

7. No

8. Blood test in a laboratory

Lesson 7

CARING FOR THE CAREGIVER

1. The Overloaded Pastor

Stephan thought things were getting better. After 20 years as pastor of a poor church in the busy city, he finally dared to hope. He had seen dictators come and go, grabbing as much as they could get from the people. He had seen the army take power. He had seen corruption in high places and violence in low places. Through it all, he preached about Jesus Christ, the Lord of all.

Poverty was still a problem for the people in his church, but it looked like the economy might be waking up. He was no expert, but he saw some factories being built in the cities. Some new shops were opening. Half the people still lacked running water, but he saw ads for cell phones and computers. Maybe some of the country's wealth was finally trickling down to the people. Not that he wanted to be rich—he was well aware that money brought lots of other problems. He was just tired of watching malnourished children playing in sewage-ridden streets. He was weary of diseases that ran wild because of poor health care. Maybe his beloved country was finally turning the corner.

And then the earth moved.

He had just walked out of the home of a sick church member. Three steps into the street and he felt like he was walking on water. He looked back to see the house crumbling. He rushed back to try to save the sick man, but there was too much debris. He called for help, but there were a dozen houses on that block in the same condition, and many people trapped inside them. He did all he could, but he couldn't reach his ailing friend.

The next few hours, days, and weeks were full of frantic activity. Church people were in great need. His flock needed him more than ever. In those first days, he rushed from place to place trying to dig out survivors. He tried to organize food and water distribution. He personally tried to contact every member of his congregation, but many were missing. He hardly had time to deal with the fact that his own house and the church building were badly damaged.

People came up to Pastor Stephan on the street with their stories and their questions. Stories of grief and survival. Questions of *why?* The pastor did his best to listen well and to give good answers, but it was getting harder and harder to care for these needy people.

His mind is flooded with pictures of tragedy. Everywhere he goes, he still hears the moaning of people in pain. Even now when he walks down a street he worries that there are living people trapped inside those piles of wood and concrete, even though his mind tells him that's impossible. *Is that a cry for help?* His wife has noticed that he has not been sleeping well for the last few weeks and awakens with the slightest noise. He realizes he no longer has the energy he used to have. He wakes up feeling tired. Sometimes he thinks the ground is rolling under his feet again. He re-lives that moment and shudders. *Just a few seconds earlier and I would have been trapped too!*

For the past month Stephan has felt more and more discouraged. He no longer wants to preach and has been thinking of resigning. He feels he is a failure as a pastor. There are so many needs that he has left unmet. His wife is worried because he rarely talks to her any more. He didn't even compliment her on the mango tart she made especially for him. She went to great lengths to find the ingredients for this specialty of hers, but he just shrugged and said it didn't taste the same. "Maybe it's all the dust," he said. "I'm just not tasting anything anymore."

 DISCUSSION QUESTIONS

1. *Why do you think Pastor Stephan is having all these problems?*

2. *Do you know any people who have become so overloaded helping others that they became very discouraged or sick? What do they say? How do they behave?*

2. How Can We Know If a Caregiver Is Overloaded?

Taking care of other people can wear us out. We can get so busy caring for others that we do not take time to care for ourselves. If we behave in some of the following ways, we may be overloaded:

- Feeling angry or sad all the time.
- Feeling tired and irritable.
- Not sleeping well.
- Having problems with relationships.
- Questioning the truth of our faith.
- Questioning God's goodness and power.
- Beginning to believe the lies of Satan.
- Becoming ill or having many accidents.
- Resenting those who need our help.
- Vividly remembering tragic events when asleep or even awake.
- Feeling the emotional pain of others so strongly it is as if it is their own pain.

If we have some of these symptoms for a long time, we need to change something in our situation. If we allow ourselves to become exhausted, we will not be able to carry on with the work God has given us.

 SMALL GROUP DISCUSSION

Have you ever felt overloaded? Describe how you felt.

3. Why Is It Difficult To Be a Caregiver?

In times of crisis, many people have problems and need to talk to someone about them, so a pastor's work increases. This is true of other church workers, lay counselors, teachers, and medical personnel as well. Caregivers may face some of the following difficulties.

A. Caregivers may have too many people to care for.

A caregiver may think he or she is indispensable to God's work and has to personally care for everyone. Or church members may think that the pastor has to do everything. They may want to talk to the pastor and no one else.

B. Caregivers can be the object of people's anger.

People who have experienced trauma are often angry. They can sometimes lash out without reason at the people around them. This can include the caregivers, even though they are only trying to help. When this happens, caregivers must recognize that the hurt person is not really angry with them. They must not take it personally.

C. Caregivers may be manipulated by people.

Some people who come with problems are not really wanting solutions. They want to blame others, but are not willing to change themselves. If the caregiver tries to confront these people about their part in the problem, they might try to change the subject. People like this can take up a lot of time. Caregivers need to discern those that really want help from those who are merely seeking attention.

D. Caregivers may find out certain things in confidence that they must tell others.

When people share their problems with a caregiver, what they say is usually held in confidence. Some things, however, cannot be kept secret. These would include illegal activities, rape, plans that would hurt someone, or plans of suicide. Those speaking to the caregiver need to understand ahead of time that these things must be reported to the authorities.

E. Caregivers may find that they enjoy being at the center of everything.

Some caregivers enjoy a sense of power over other people's lives. It may make them feel needed when otherwise they are lacking in confidence. Sometimes helping others is a way of avoiding looking at one's own problems. These are not good reasons for helping others. The caregiver may need to stop and look at his or her own motivation for helping others. Are they really focused on serving God and others? Are their motives pure?

F. Caregivers may ignore how they really feel inside.

Caregivers may think they should be strong enough to bear heavy burdens without complaining or becoming angry. But if they deny their own feelings of anger and sadness and fear, they run the risk of serious spiritual and emotional exhaustion. This may even cause them to be less helpful or cause them to unintentionally harm the ones they want to help.

G. Caregivers may neglect their own families.

Caring for people takes lots of time. Caregivers can easily spend so much time with others that their own spouses and children are neglected. This will eventually cause serious problems. A spouse may become depressed or angry. The children may feel angry that this parent has time for everyone else but has no time for them. The caregiver may no longer be at home enough to discipline the children properly. The relationship between husband, wife, and children may become distant, leaving caregivers feeling lonely in their own home.

 SMALL GROUP DISCUSSION

What difficulties have you experienced as you have cared for people?

4. How Can Caregivers Take Care of Themselves?

 DISCUSSION QUESTION

(Hold up a machete and sharpening file.) What will happen to this machete if I never sharpen it? Is the time I take to sharpen it wasted or well-used?

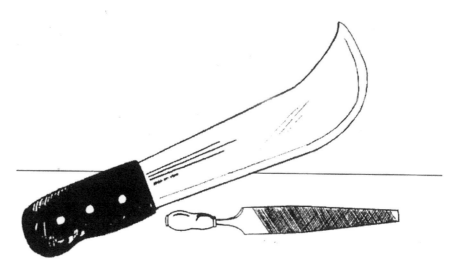

Taking Time to Sharpen the Machete

We are God's instruments for good in the world (2 Timothy 2:21). If instruments are not cared for, they will break down and lose their usefulness. Just as we must stop using a machete to clean it and sharpen it, so we must stop and care for ourselves. Then we will be able to take care of others.

When we listen to people's problems, we absorb some of their pain and carry it with us. When we listen to many people, the burden of all their pain can be very heavy, much heavier than any one of them bears individually. We have to be careful not to be crushed by it.

A. Let God care for you.

 SMALL GROUP EXERCISE

1. Read I Kings 19:3-8. What did God do for Elijah when he was tired and discouraged?

1 Kings 19:3-8: Elijah was afraid and ran for his life. When he came to Beersheba in Judah, he left his servant there, while he himself went a day's journey into the desert. He came to a broom tree, sat down under it and prayed that he might die. "I have had enough, Lord," he said. "Take my life; I am no better than my ancestors." Then he lay down under the tree and fell asleep. All at once an angel touched him and said, "Get up and eat."

2. Read Mark 6:30-32. What did Jesus tell the disciples after they had finished ministering to many people?

Mark 6:30-32 The apostles gathered around Jesus and reported to him all they had done and taught. Then, because so many people were coming and going that they did not even have a chance to eat, he said to them, "Come with me by yourselves to a quiet place and get some rest." So they went away by themselves in a boat to a solitary place.

God has promised to comfort us, help us and be strong for us when we are overwhelmed. He understands that we are weak. Even Jesus got tired and sad and felt troubled. The Bible gives us many examples of God's servants who were so tired that they could not continue their work. God gave them special care at that time. Take time in prayer to know God's love and care for you (Psalms 35:27).

B. Share your burdens with others.

Have regular times for sharing and prayer with a small group or another person. Share with other caregivers or mature Christians. In the same way that people who have experienced trauma need to talk it out, caregivers need to share their burdens with someone (Galatians 6:2).

C. Share the workload with others.

 DISCUSSION QUESTION

Read Exodus 18:13-23. What was Moses' problem? How did he solve it?

Exodus 18:13-23: The next day Moses took his seat to serve as judge for the people, and they stood around him from morning till evening. When his father-in-law saw all that Moses was doing for the people, he said, "What is this you are doing for the people? Why do you alone sit as judge, while all these people stand around you from morning till evening?" Moses answered him, "Because the people come to me to seek God's will. Whenever they have a dispute, it is brought to me, and I decide between the parties and inform them of God's decrees and laws." Moses' father-in-law replied, "What you are doing is not good. You and these people who come to you will only wear yourselves out. The work is too heavy for you; you cannot handle it alone. Listen now to me and I will give you some advice, and may God be with you. You must be the people's representative before God and bring their disputes to him. Teach them the decrees and laws, and show them the way to live and the duties they are to perform. But select capable men from all the people—men who fear God, trustworthy men who hate dishonest gain—and appoint them as officials over thousands, hundreds, fifties and tens. Have them serve as judges for the people at all times, but have them bring every difficult case to you; the simple cases they can decide themselves. That will make your load lighter, because they will share it with you. If you do this and God so commands, you will be able to stand the strain, and all these people will go home satisfied."

Sharing the workload means, first of all, giving up some of the control of your ministry. Others will do things differently than you do, and you will no longer be at the center of everything that happens.

Identify others in the church who are mature and who are gifted in helping others. It is good to have a balanced team of people: men and women, from different ages and ethnic groups (Romans 12:4-8). Train them how to help others. By doing this, you help people respect their ability to help others. Your satisfaction then comes from training them well and seeing them succeed.

If people from other churches are coming to you, explain what is happening to their pastors or priests so that they don't think that you are trying to steal their members from them. Train these pastors and priests in how to help people with wounded hearts.

Help church members understand that people besides the pastor can help them. In some religions only the religious leader can do the work, but in Christianity, church members can minister to one another. Help church members understand that you will be able to work better if you can take time to "sharpen your machete."

D. Take time away from the situation.

Find opportunities to rest and get away from the difficulties and pain. Jesus and his disciples did. "There were so many people coming and going that Jesus and his disciples didn't even have time to eat. So he said to them, 'Let us go off by ourselves to some place where we will be alone and you can rest a while'" (Mark 6:31). Sometimes it takes several days of rest to begin to release the burden.

Spouses and children are part of the ministry God gives us. They are not a barrier to it. Caregivers need to reserve time for their wife and children. In some cases, a family retreat or holiday might be appropriate.

E. Take care of your physical body.

- Get exercise daily. Exercise releases stress.

- Get enough sleep. Adults need 7-8 hours per night.

- Eat a good, nourishing diet. Inexpensive peanuts, eggs, grains, fruits and vegetables are sometimes available, even if money for food is limited. Don't become so busy with the work that you forget to eat. You need good food to be strong physically. (And even if others around you are hungry, you need to eat properly in order to minister to them effectively. Share with others, but provide for yourself as well.)

✖ CLOSING EXERCISE

In small groups, describe your workload. How can you care for yourself and your family as you care for others?

Response:
TAKING YOUR PAIN TO
THE CROSS

PREPARING FOR THIS EXERCISE

Instructions for Leaders

This exercise should be done toward the end of the seminar, after people have been thinking about their heart wounds and feel ready to share their pain with God and others. It must be done in a way that people know that they will not be criticized, and that what they share will not be used against them. It is not a magic ritual, but a symbolic way to experience God beginning to heal our pain. It is often done as an evening session.

To prepare for this exercise, the leaders need to make a cross out of wood and get paper and pens for everyone. They will also need matches and a place outside to burn the papers. It is very important that the papers burn without a lot of difficulty or danger, as that would distract from the meaning of the experience.

If it's not possible to make a cross, the leaders need to devise some other symbol of the cross. A cross drawn on a box could suffice. If paper is not available, or if people are not literate, other items that can burn, like small sticks, could be used to symbolize their pain. This might also be necessary in areas where people are afraid their security might be at risk if these things were written down even for a moment.

If the papers are to be nailed to the cross, leaders will need to have a hammer and nails. If the papers are to be put in a box at the foot of the cross, they'll need a box that is ready for this.

The large group will be divided into small groups of three during the exercise for a time of sharing their deepest pain. The leaders will need to decide in advance how best to divide up the group. Sometimes it is important to keep men with men, pastors with pastors, and women with women. Children should be grouped with at least one adult. In some situations, leaders may allow participants to choose who they will meet with.

It may be good to talk about the experience the next day, to discuss how people felt about it, and how they could do this with other groups in their churches. Healing takes time. This ceremony can be an important part of the process of healing. It will not necessarily heal all hurts instantaneously. Yet when people trust each other enough to share their deepest pain, and when they hear each other's pain, healing begins to happen.

1. Identify the Wounds of Your Heart

We are taught in Scripture that Jesus not only came to bear our sins, but also to bear our pain. Isaiah 53:3-4 says, "We despised him and rejected him; he endured suffering and pain. . . . Surely he took up our infirmities and carried our sorrows, yet we considered him stricken by God, smitten by him, and afflicted."

Isaiah 61:1-3 says:

> The Sovereign LORD has filled me with his Spirit.
> He has chosen me and sent me
> to bring good news to the poor,
> to heal the broken-hearted,
> to announce release to captives
> and freedom to those in prison.
> He has sent me to proclaim
> that the time has come
> when the LORD will save his people
> and defeat their enemies.
> He has sent me to comfort all who mourn,
> to give to those who mourn in Zion
> joy and gladness instead of grief,
> a song of praise instead of sorrow.
> They will be like trees
> that the LORD himself has planted.
> they will all do what is right,
> and God will be praised for what he has done.

Jesus felt the full burden of human pain and sinfulness. Jesus knows the pain that is in our hearts and we need to bring it to him so he can heal us. In this exercise, we will experience bringing our pains to the cross.

A. Write down your worst pain.

Ask God to show you the painful things that are buried deep in your heart. Which are the ones that are most painful? Which memories do you not like to think about? Write these down. We will bring these to the cross and burn them later, so no one will ever see what you have written.

Be as specific as possible. You should write down the worst things that you remember such as:

- Terrible things that have happened to you or been done to you.
- Terrible things you have seen happen to others, or bad dreams you have had.
- Terrible things you have heard about that have happened to others.
- Terrible things that you may have done to others.

This should take about 20 minutes. It is helpful for people to be alone as they do this.

B. Share your pain in small groups.

Divide into groups of three. Each person should be encouraged to share something he or she has written down. The other two should listen without criticizing or offering advice. Share openly but don't dwell on the violent parts unnecessarily. Be sure all three have an opportunity to share.

If people are not able to write, they could make a mark on paper, or have someone else write for them, or use a stick to represent their pain. At the end decide what things the group would like to share with the large group. Take about 30 minutes for this.

C. The small groups share with the large group.

In the large group, each person should be encouraged to share briefly the pain that he or she has experienced. Be specific, but do not tell the whole story again. For example, you might say, "I saw my father being killed" or "I got beaten up by a gang of looters."

When everyone who wants to share has done so, the leader asks, "What can we do with these pains?" Then he reads Isaiah 53:4-6:

But he endured the suffering that should have been ours,
the pain that we should have borne.
All the while we thought that his suffering
was punishment sent by God.
But because of our sins he was wounded,
beaten because of the evil we did.
We are healed by the punishment he suffered,
made whole by the blows he received.
All of us were like sheep that were lost,
each of us going his own way.
But the LORD made the punishment fall on him,
the punishment all of us deserved.

2. Bring Your Wounds and Pain to Jesus

A. Talk to Jesus about your pain.

Take some time to bring your pain to Jesus. Tell him exactly what it is: for example, anger, sadness, loneliness, or feeling abandoned. Empty your soul. Let any emotions you feel about the pain come out.

B. Bring your pain to the cross.

Bring the paper on which you wrote your pain to the cross. Nail it to the cross, or put it in the box at the foot of the cross. As you do, say, "I'm handing over my suffering to Jesus who died on the cross for me."

C. Burn the papers.

When all the papers have been deposited, take them outside and burn them. This shows that the suffering we have experienced has become like ashes (Isaiah 61:3). This is a stage in knowing God's healing.

Afterwards, people should pray for the person on either side of them that Jesus will continue to heal his or her wounded hearts.

3. Share the Good Things God Has Done

Invite some people to share the ways that they have seen God at work, even in the midst of their problems.

Thank God and praise him in words and songs because he is healing the wounds in our hearts.

Lesson 9

HOW CAN WE FORGIVE OTHERS?

1. Real and Fake Forgiveness

Act out the following short skits:

1. Pòl chita ak Bèna zanmi li. Li di l, "Semenn pase a nèg yo bay pou Simon an fè m wont. Devan tout lòt pastè yo li di mwen pa konn preche. Se pa ti mal bagay sa a fè m mal jouk jodia." Bèna fè yon deplase, Simon rantre. Simon di, Souple padone m pou sa m te di semenn pase a." Epi Pòl di, "Pa gen pwoblèm non, sa w ou te di pat grav, anyen pa deranje."

2. Pastè Kristòf ap pale ak Elyezè, yon fidèl legliz la. Elyezè di, "M eseye padone papa m pou jan li maltrete m lè m te piti men sa difisil pou mwen." Pastè Kristòf di, "Enben ou dwe fè yon jan pou bliye bagay sa a, si ou pa bliye l ou pa ka di ou padone papa w."

3. Lisyen te fè klas lekòl didimanch gran moun yo dimanch pase paske pwofesè yo wa pat la. Seza, yon elèv nan klas la te fè yon gwo diskisyon pou granmesi. Se te yon bagay deryen wi. Sa te nwi Lisyen anpil. Msye te vrèman jennen pou sa Seza te fè a. Pita nan semenn nan, Lisyen te kwaze ak pwofesè li te kenbe pou li a. Pwofesè a te di l mèsi dèske li te kenbe pou li. Lisyen pale li de lobo Seza te fè nan klas la epi li di "M pa mande Bondye pou m janm kenbe pou ou nan klas sa a ankò!" Pwofesè a te mande Lisyen pou yo al chita ak Seza pou yo ka rezoud malantandi a. Yo chita pale e Lisyen te esplike Seza jan li te santi l apre diskisyon ki te rive nan klas la. Li te esplike jan li te nwi dèske li pat ka bay yon repons korèk, jan li te anbarase. Seza te di jan li regret sak te pase a. Li te mande Lisyen padon. Lisyen te padone li ak tout kè li.

DISCUSSION QUESTION

Which of these situations show real forgiveness? How is it different from the others?

2. Forgiveness Is Not . . .

- Saying the offense didn't matter.
- Saying we were not hurt by what the person did (Ephesians 4:25).
- Acting as if the event never happened.
- Dependent on the offender apologizing first or changing his or her behavior (Romans 5:8).
- Letting the person who did wrong avoid the consequences of the action (Romans 13:2).
- Letting the offender hurt us or other innocent people again.
- Trusting a person again right after they hurt us.

3. What Is Forgiveness?

A. Forgiveness involves bringing the pain to Christ.

Forgiving someone means that we recognize that the person has wronged us, and we accept the pain his or her sin has caused us. We bring our pain to the cross and release it to Jesus. When Jesus heals our pain, then we will be able to forgive those who have hurt us. If we think forgiving is too hard for us to do, we are right. God is the only one who can enable us to forgive.

B. Complete forgiveness of a deep hurt takes time.

Forgiveness does not happen all at once. It is like a journey where we lose our way repeatedly. We start to forgive, but then we circle back as we remember the hurt of the offense. Then we forgive again a little more thoroughly, and gradually we make our way to complete forgiveness.

When we forgive someone, we will still remember what happened. At first, we may also feel the pain associated with it. When this happens, we need to continue to take the parts that hurt to Jesus. The commitment to forgive often comes before the feelings of forgiveness, and sometimes long before. As we bring our hurt to Jesus over and over, eventually we will no longer feel any pain when we remember the event. Then we can know that our forgiveness is complete.

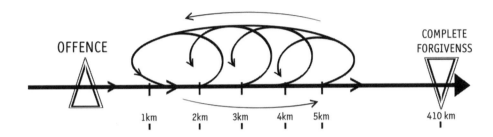

OFFENCE

COMPLETE FORGIVENSS

1km 2km 3km 4km 5km   410 km

The Cycle of Forgiveness

To forgive someone does not mean that we trust that person immediately. Just because we have forgiven a person does not mean that he or she has changed. Even if that person has changed, our trust is broken and will take time to rebuild. Little by little as we have good experiences with that person, we will begin to trust him or her again. But it may take a long time before we can trust completely, if ever.

C. Forgiveness does not depend on what the other person does.

Often we are unwilling to forgive until the offender has apologized to us. Or we want to see that the person has changed the behavior before we forgive him or her. Like Jesus, we need to forgive people, even if they are not sorry about the evil they have done. On the cross Jesus said, "Forgive them, Father! They don't know what they are doing" (Luke 23:34).

D. Forgiveness still requires the offender to face the consequences of his or her act.

Forgiving someone does not mean that the person will not be punished if he or she has done wrong things. By forgiving, we allow God to judge and take revenge (Romans 12:19-21). He can do this much better than we can. God has also given national and local leaders the job of punishing criminals and protecting the innocent (Roman 13:1-4). Even though we have forgiven someone, it may be necessary to bring that person to justice, for the good of society.

Even though we have forgiven our enemies, we should defend the innocent from violent or evil people if they try to harm them again.

Forgiveness also requires the offender to pay back what he has taken, if possible. Some things, like a person's life or a woman's virginity, can never really be repaid. But if someone has stolen chickens, he should pay them back. Sin must be paid for, even if it involves great expense. God gave us the model to follow when Jesus paid for the sins of the whole world on the cross, (and he was completely innocent).

 **DISCUSSION QUESTION**

How are the biblical ideas about forgiveness similar to the ideas of our culture? How are they different?

4. Why Does God Want Us to Forgive Other People?

A. Forgiveness frees us from anger and bitterness.

If we do not forgive someone who has offended us, we are the ones who suffer. Our anger allows Satan a way into our hearts (Ephesians 4:26-27; 2 Corinthians 2:10-11). We become slaves of our anger and bitterness, and they begin to destroy us. Refusing to forgive can make us physically ill with headaches, stomach ulcers, or heart problems. It may make us become as violent and evil as those who offended us. Forgiveness releases us from all this. We forgive for our own good.

Forgiveness Sets Us Free from the Chains of Bitterness

If we do not forgive others, we pass our hatred on to our children. This can result in cycles of revenge and violence between groups which can go on for generations. Only forgiveness can break the cycle. Forgiveness also allows us to begin the healing process.

B. Forgiveness allows us to receive God's forgiveness.

God's forgiveness depends on our forgiving those who offend us. Matthew 6:14-15 says, "If you forgive others the wrongs they have done to you, your Father in heaven will also forgive you. But if you do not forgive others, then your Father will not forgive the wrongs you have done." (See also Mark 11:25.)

C. Forgiveness shows that we understand Christ's sacrifice and our salvation.

When we understand how much we have offended God by our sinfulness, and how Jesus forgave us even before we repented (1 John 4:10), any offense we have experienced will seem small. We will want to extend that same forgiveness to others (Ephesians 4:32; Matthew 18:21-35).

D. Forgiveness allows us to be reconciled with those who have offended us.

Until we forgive those who have offended us, our relationship with them will suffer. Forgiveness makes it possible for our relationship with them to be restored. Full restoration, however, requires repentance and forgiveness on both sides.

E. Forgiveness can change the person who offended us.

Forgiving someone may be the start of God bringing that person to repent. In Acts 7, as Stephen was dying, he forgave those who were killing him. One of those people was Saul, who later became Paul the apostle (Acts 7:60-8:1).

 SMALL GROUP DISCUSSION

1. *What do you find the hardest thing about forgiving someone? What has helped you the most to forgive others?*

2. *What traditions do we have that help us to repent and forgive others? What traditions do we have that hinder us from repenting and forgiving?*

5. What If We Are the Ones Who Have Caused the Offense?

A. How do we repent?

- We allow God's spirit to show us how much our sin hurts him and others. This may make us sad and even weep as God breaks our hearts (James 4:8-9). This sorrow can be good for us. "For God can use sorrow in our lives to help us turn away from sin and seek salvation. We will never regret that kind of sorrow. But sorrow without repentance is the kind that results in death" (2 Corinthians 7:10, NLT). Both Peter and Judas were sad that they had denied Jesus, but Peter's sorrow brought him closer to God; Judas' led him to kill himself.

- We take responsibility for what we have done and clearly state our sin (Proverbs 28:13; Psalms 32:3-5).

- We ask God to forgive us for the sin, and then accept that he has done so (1 John 1:9).

- We ask those we have offended to forgive us, without defending ourselves or blaming them (James 5:16). We should ask forgiveness in such a way that all those affected by our sin are aware of our repentance. For example, if we have insulted someone in front of others, then we should ask forgiveness in front of the other people as well.

- If we have repented in our hearts, we will show it by the way we act (Acts 26:20b).

- Repentance may involve paying back what was taken (Numbers 5:5-7).

B. How can the church help people repent?

Church leaders are charged to watch over the spiritual life of their members (1 Peter 5:2-3). If a member is sinning, and will not listen to those who talk to him about his sin, the church leaders should talk to him (Matthew 18:15-17; Galatians 6:1).

If the person refuses to repent even after repeated efforts, he must be excluded from the church (1 Corinthians 5:4-5:11). This is a very painful process. It is done to protect the church's purity (1 Corinthians 5:67), and to bring the person to repentance. Even after he is excluded from the group, the leaders should continue to try to help him to come to repentance.

 **DISCUSSION QUESTION**

As a church, how do we deal with members when they sin? Has this helped them to repent?

✗ CLOSING EXERCISE

Omit these exercises if the group will be going on to the final ceremony.

1. *Have one person read each of the following verses aloud and give the main point.*

   Ephesians 4:32: Be kind and compassionate to one another, forgiving each other, just as in Christ God forgave you.

   Matthew 18:35: This is how my heavenly Father will treat each of you unless you forgive your brother from your heart.

   Matthew 18:21-22: Then Peter came to Jesus and asked, "Lord, how many times shall I forgive my brother when he sins against me? Up to seven times?" Jesus answered, "I tell you, not seven times, but seventy-seven times."

   Romans 12:14: Bless those who persecute you; bless and do not curse.

2. *Take five minutes in silence to ask God to show you any sins that you need to repent of. Confess those sins to God and receive his forgiveness. At the end of the time, read 1 John 1:9 aloud.*

1 John 1:9: If we confess our sins, he is faithful and just and will forgive us our sins and purify us from all unrighteousness.

3. *Take another five minutes to reflect on any people that you need to forgive. Ask God to help you forgive them.*

4. *Share together what God has shown you about forgiveness.*

5. *Praise God, in words and in song, that he forgives us and enables us to forgive others.*

HOW CAN WE LIVE AS CHRISTIANS IN THE MIDST OF CONFLICT?

Use this lesson if you have ethnic or cultural conflict tension in your area. Use it after the lesson on forgiveness, and before the final ceremony.

1. The Story of Jonah and Rene

Jonah was a faithful Christian, a leader in his church. He even taught a Bible class there. Everyone was impressed with how loving and caring he was. But he had a deep secret. He didn't like mulattos.

It bothered him that he had to slave away in a factory while people with half his intelligence were owning shops and teaching school and, well, running the country. They had their fashion and their food and their music. It wasn't just skin color; it was an attitude. Arrogance! There were some dark-skinned people who started to make some money and sort of turned into mulattos, as far as Jonah was concerned. He didn't waste a lot of time thinking about it. It was just the way things were.

Every day on the street of the capital city, Jonah passed a mulatto man, Rene, who worked in a government office. Rene wasn't extremely wealthy, but he dressed well. He was also a genuine Christian, though he went to a church on the other side of town. Of course Jonah didn't know this. They just walked past each other with nothing more than a glance.

The earthquake broke down all sorts of walls. Jonah was coming home from the factory and saw buildings pan-caking around him. He jumped to help, pulling debris away to free those underneath. There was one house where the entry was blocked by a concrete slab. Jonah couldn't budge it by himself, but another man saw his struggle and joined him. Together, they heaved and heaved, and finally moved it aside. A grateful family ran out into the street. Jonah turned and extended a hand to the man who helped with the slab. "We did it, brother."

It was Rene. "Yes, we did. Thank God!"

In that moment the two men saw a glimmer of faith in each other's eyes. Jonah began to think that maybe mulattos weren't so arrogant after all. Rene was revising his own racial ideas.

"Let's go and see what else we can do," Jonah said. "With God's help."

 SMALL GROUP DISCUSSION

1. Do you think these two men could ever become friends?

2. Do you think attitudes of prejudice are common in your culture?

3. How could we begin to change this?

2. What Are Some Causes of Conflict between Groups?

A. Desire for resources

At the base of every conflict is the desire to have something so strongly we are willing to fight for it (James 4:1-3). We may fight over land or water, for example. We may be greedy and want more than our share of the resources, or fearful that others will take what we have from us.

B. Ineffective or unjust governments

God has put governments in place to see that people receive justice (Romans 13:1-4). When governments do not do their job and there is widespread suffering, at some point people rebel. In times of political instability, old conflicts between groups re-surface because there is no one to stop them.

C. Trouble-makers

Some individuals, like Hitler, can single-handedly stir up whole nations to war. The newspapers and radio can also fan the flames of hatred. Soon people are killing each other without really understanding why, and the cycle of violence begins. This can also happen in communities. Once it is started, it can only be stopped by radical forgiveness.

D. A heritage of prejudice

Children inherit prejudice and hatred for other groups from their parents. Whenever we think, "The people from the other group are always . . .," we are expressing a prejudice. Prejudices portray all members of the other group as if they are the same, and all bad. Prejudices keep people from ever finding out what the other group is really like. If they did, they would discover that their prejudices are not accurate. There are both good and bad people in every group.

In times of conflict, all the problems are blamed on the other group. In some conflicts, the other group is portrayed as if the people aren't even human.

Meanwhile, people see their own group as superior, and entitled to certain things, like land or status. For example, one group may feel entitled to special respect and service from another group.

 DISCUSSION QUESTIONS

1. *Are there conflicts in your community or country? What are the roots of these conflicts?*

2. *Are there any prejudices you have inherited about another group? Can you think of any evidence that would show these ideas are not true?*

3. *How do others describe your group? What evidence might they have for this description?*

3. How Can We Live as Christians in the Midst of Conflict?

 DISCUSSION QUESTION

Why is it difficult to live as Christians in the midst of conflict?

God calls Christians to be salt and light, bringing the good news of Jesus Christ into evil and dark situations (Matthew 5:13-16; Philippians 2:1416). Christians are to have their minds transformed by Christ. This means that they will react differently from non-Christians (Romans 12:1-2). This is the path of blessing, but it is not easy. It will need a daily, intentional decision.

A. We must realize God's sovereignty.

Matthew 10:28-31 says, "Do not be afraid of those who kill the body but cannot kill the soul; rather be afraid of God, who can destroy both body and soul in hell. For only a penny you can buy two sparrows, yet not one sparrow falls to the ground without your Father's consent. As for you, even the hairs of your head have all been counted. So do not be afraid; you are worth much more than many sparrows!"

Not even a small bird dies without God knowing it. We can trust that whatever happens to us is God's will. He will use it for our good (Romans 8:28).

Even when evil is done, it is within God's larger plan. We must look beyond the evildoer to see the hand of God in the situation. Both Joseph and Jesus suffered, but God used their suffering for good (Genesis 45:5-7; Acts 3:13-15). God is at work, even through people's evil intentions.

We must realize that our lives are not our own. God knows the date of our death before we're even born (Psalms 139:15-16). If we have been spared while others have died, it is because God still has a purpose for our lives (Esther 4:13-14; 2 Thessalonians 1:11-12).

B. We must be prepared to give up everything but Christ.

In times of conflict, everything that defined who we are may be taken from us: our family members, our homes, our possessions, our work, our own lives. Only Christ can never be taken from us. 1 Peter 1:3-6 says, "Let us give thanks to the God and Father of our Lord Jesus Christ! Because of his great mercy he gave us new life by raising Jesus Christ from death. This fills us with a living hope, and so we look forward to possessing the rich blessings that God keeps for his people. He keeps them for you in heaven, where they cannot decay or spoil or fade away. They are for you, who through faith are kept safe by God's power for the salvation which is ready to be revealed at the end of time."

We must voluntarily give up the cultural prejudices we grew up with. Old ways of judging others must go; they are worldly and cause divisions. 2 Corinthians 5:16-18 says, "No longer, then, do we judge anyone by human standards. Even if at one time we judged Christ according to human standards, we no longer do so. Anyone who is joined to Christ is a new being; the old is gone, the new has come. All this is done by God, who through Christ changed us from enemies into his friends and gave us the task of making others his friends also."

Our only desire must be to know Christ, and to help others know him (Galatians 2:20; Philippians 1:21; 3:8). Christ has redeemed us from all of the evil in our past (1 Peter 1:17-19).

We must give up any rights we think we might have as members of our group. God has no favorites; all people are accepted equally by him (Acts 10:34; Romans 2:9-11). We now belong to a new nation with other believers where everyone is equal (1 Peter 2:9; Ephesians 2:18-22; Revelation 5:9-10). Christ provided the model for us to follow when he gave up his rights as God to save us (Philippians 2:5-11).

Everything we give up for Christ will be rewarded one hundred times (Matthew 19:29; Luke 9:23), but the process is not easy.

C. We must not take revenge, but show love.

Romans 12:19-21 says, "Never take revenge, my friends, but instead let God's anger do it. For the scripture says, 'I will take revenge, I will pay back, says the Lord.' Instead, as the scripture says: 'If your enemies are hungry, feed them; if they are thirsty, give them a drink; for by doing this you will make them burn with shame.' Do not let evil defeat you; instead, conquer evil with good."

As Christians, we no longer have the responsibility to take revenge for the wrongs done to us or our families. We are to show love and allow God to punish others (Matthew 5:38-42). Revenge does not bring peace to our hearts or bring back what was lost. It only perpetuates the violence.

Each human life is sacred because it reflects God's image (Genesis 1:27). We are not to destroy or mistreat it, but we can defend our lives and the lives of others.

God works through governments to bring justice, punish evil doers, and protect the innocent. "Everyone must obey state authorities, because no authority exists without God's permission, and the existing authorities have been put there by God. Whoever opposes the existing authority opposes what God has ordered; and anyone who does so will bring judgment on himself. . . . They are God's servants and carry out God's punishment on those who do evil" (Romans 13:1-2,4b).

Even when governments are unjust and ineffective, we should not take the law into our own hands. The most powerful thing Jesus did was to make himself completely vulnerable to his enemies on the cross (1 Peter 2:21-23). People like Gandhi in India and Martin Luther King in the United States have challenged governments by standing against evil without using violence. These movements have resulted in correcting widespread injustice more effectively than a violent reaction could have, and those involved were not guilty of shedding blood.

D. We must receive strength from God.

In times of conflict, we need to stay close to God. We should read the Bible regularly (2 Timothy 3:16-17; Romans 12:1-2). We need to spend time in prayer bringing our wounds and concerns to God, and receiving his peace in our hearts (Philippians 4:6-7). Writing a lament about our experiences might help us to express our pain to God.

We may need to spend time away from the situation "on the mountain" with God to restore our souls (Mark 6:31, 45-46). The Holy Spirit will help us, even when we are weak (Acts 1:8; 2 Corinthians 12:9-10).

We need to meet with other Christians, share our pains, and pray for one another (Hebrews 10:25; James 5:16). We should be careful not to talk about the situation in ways that sow more seeds of bitterness (I Corinthians 14:26).

4. How Can We Help Bring Reconciliation?

 EXERCISE

Prepare a skit in which two groups go through the motions of reconciliation but are not really reconciled.

A. We must become a bridge between the groups in conflict.

God created us to be social beings. By nature, we want and need to belong to a group. In times of conflict, we may need to sacrifice that need to belong and become a bridge between the two groups in conflict. For example, we should share food and resources with those in need, no matter which side they are on. This may put our lives at risk. Our "enemies" may want to hurt us because we are their enemies. But our brothers may also want to hurt us because we have befriended the enemy. Close family members may condemn us.

God calls us to love our enemies (Matthew 5:43-48). When we do this, we no longer have any enemies. All people become our brothers and sisters.

If we do not know any other peace-makers in the situation, we may be alone with God as our only friend (Matthew 5:9). We may well feel we are aliens in this world (1 Peter 1:2; Hebrews 11:13-16).

As a bridge between the two groups, we need to try to understand the pain that each side of the conflict has experienced from their perspective. Then we can help each side understand the pain of the other, to give up their prejudice and view them as humans.

If we hear too much from one side and we begin to see only their point of view, we need to spend time with the other side to recover perspective.

B. We must lead people to Christ so that they find healing and repent of their sins.

God has given us the ministry of reconciling people to Christ (2 Corinthians 5:17-20). Where there is conflict, nearly everyone has wounds of the heart. These must be brought to Christ so he can heal the pain. Where people have sinned against others, they must repent and ask God and those they have hurt to forgive them.

C. We must help people repent of the sins of their group.

The worst things that happen in the world are caused not by individuals, but by groups: ethnic groups, governments, churches. Even if we were not involved personally in causing suffering, as members of our group, we need to repent before God for the suffering our group has caused. Then we need to ask forgiveness of those we have hurt on behalf of our group. In the Bible, Daniel, Nehemiah, and Ezra all did this on behalf of their people (Daniel 9:49; Nehemiah 9:2-36; Ezra 9:5-15; Leviticus 26:40). There are also many current examples of people doing this today: Americans asking forgiveness of Native Americans, Germans asking forgiveness of the Dutch for the suffering they inflicted on them during World War II, South African Whites asking forgiveness of Blacks. Usually, when one group repents and asks forgiveness, the other group repents as well, and reconciliation follows.

D. Groups must discuss their problems openly and find solutions.

When the pain in people's hearts is healed, then the real problems that started the conflict must be addressed. People need to work together, give and take, and find a solution that is fair and acceptable to all.

No problems are too small to need attention. No matter how small, they can become big if they are not solved.

E. Celebrate Christ and the unity he brings.

When Christ has broken down barriers between us, we need to celebrate and praise him together (Ephesians 2:14). He is Lord. He sets us free from the lies and traps of the enemy.

✖ CLOSING EXERCISE

Read this story about ethnic tensions in the early church. Then act it out. Divide into three groups: the homeland Jews, the foreign Jews, and the apostles. The homeland Jews and the foreign Jews should present their case to the apostles in turn. Then the apostles can give their decision. Finally discuss the questions at the end of the story.

Over five hundred years before Jesus came, the powerful nations of Assyria, Babylon, and Persia conquered Israel. To keep Israel from becoming strong again, they took most of the people into exile to live in other countries. By the time Jesus was born, many Jews had lived outside their homeland for hundreds of years. They spoke Greek, the common language of the day, and lived like Greek people, but they were pious Jews who continued to worship the Lord God. They made trips to their homeland when they could, and believed it was good to be buried there. Older couples liked to move back to Israel so that when they died, they would be buried there. Often the husband died first, leaving his widow in need of someone to provide for her.

Meanwhile, the Jews who stayed in Israel through the years continued to speak their own language and practice their cultural traditions. Life was hard for them, but they persevered. And they felt that because they had never left their land or traditions, they were better in God's eyes. They looked down on the foreign Jews.

One of their traditions was to care for widows. The tithes that they offered to God were used to feed the Levites, aliens, fatherless and widows (Deuteronomy 26:12). None of the other cultures at the time took care of widows like the Jews in Israel did. Out of obedience to God, they took care of the foreign Jewish widows just like they took care of their own. There were so many foreign Jewish widows that the homeland Jews had a hard time caring for them.

In the early church, it wasn't long before the tensions between the homeland Jews and the foreign Jews became apparent. The foreign Jews complained that their widows were not being given their share when the food supplies were handed out each day (Acts 6:1-7). The apostles called a meeting to address the problem openly. They recognized that these ethnic tensions could destroy the church. So they had the group choose seven men to deal with the problem. At least one of these men, Nicolaus, was a foreign Jew from Antioch. They dealt with the problem, and the church continued to grow. The love between foreign Jewish Christians and homeland Jewish Christians was a strong testimony to those outside the church.

Over and over again, the differences between the foreign Jews and homeland Jews caused tensions in the church. Each time, the apostles took the initiative early on, discussed the problem openly, and worked out a solution that was acceptable to all (Acts 15, for example). And the church grew.

 ## DISCUSSION QUESTIONS

1. What were the historical causes of the conflict in Acts 6:1-7?

2. How did the church leaders keep the ethnic tensions from ruining the church?

3. Do you have ethnic tensions in your own church? Discuss the causes and possible solutions.

4. Acknowledge any prejudices your group may have. Pray and ask God to deliver you from them.

5. Pray for your enemies (1 Peter 4:8).

Lesson 11

LOOKING AHEAD

1. A Look Ahead

Many stories have been told in these lessons. These stories were composites of several different people. They are based on real reports from people like you. Surely you know people like Pastor Andre, Jean and Marie, Jonah and Rene. Maybe you are like one of these characters.

But in this final lesson, there's no story to tell, just a challenge to give. We're talking about the future. That chapter—of life—hasn't been written yet. Yet it's clear that you're a main character. What are you going to do?

Rebuilding. That's what everyone is talking about, and some of it is even happening. Slowly. But you know there is more to rebuild than just walls and roofs. People's hearts need to heal. And that's something that you can help with. Construction companies will send out the bulldozers and cranes to put buildings up again. And the clinics will gradually get up and running to care for people's physical needs. But you are at the forefront of the most important rebuilding of all.

How will you prepare your people for the difficult process of rebuilding the city, their lives, and their hearts?

 DISCUSSION QUESTION

As you look ahead to the next few years, how do you feel? Do you have hope, or do you think there will be more trouble?

2. Why Should We Prepare for the Future?

God's word says, "A prudent man sees danger and takes refuge, but the simple keep going and suffer for it" (Proverbs 22:3). God has given us intelligence and common sense and he expects us to use them. Church leaders are responsible before God to lead and look after their church congregations (Acts 20:26-31; 1 Peter 1:4; Jeremiah 23:1).

People in the middle of a crisis often don't have the ability to think in a clear way. If a decision has been made beforehand when there was time to study what God teaches, then it is much easier to do the right thing when the crisis comes. For example, if a community lives near a volcano, or in an area subject to flooding, plans can be made as a community as to what could be done to help prepare for a flood or a volcano eruption. How could your people prepare for another earthquake?

Sometimes government officials may think that the church leaders are getting involved with politics when they discuss this type of preparation with their congregations. Depending on the local situation, it may be good to talk with local officials about this. Indeed, they should be involved in contingency plans for a village or a community, if possible.

There are two areas of preparation that are important: practical and mental/ spiritual.

3. How Can We Prepare Practically?

 DISCUSSION QUESTION

In groups of four, imagine the following situation: Your family is told that within 30 minutes they must leave their homes forever. They can only take what they can carry. Make a list of the most important items to take and share this with the whole group.

Some things that might be important to take:

- Medicines

- Food, including salt

- Water

- Matches
- Cooking pot
- Identity papers
- Knife and/or machete
- Radio and batteries
- Bible
- Extra clothes

Could you gather these items and put them in a bag near the door, in case you have 30 seconds to leave, rather than 30 minutes?

The church leaders also need to think about church belongings and church documents. How would these be protected in case of another disaster?

4. How Can We Communicate When Trouble Comes?

A. With our families

Each family should openly discuss this, even with the children: If this sort of thing happens again, where will you go? How will you find each other? Decide on a meeting place if the family gets separated and discuss different routes to get there. It is very important that even very small children are capable of saying their name and their family name. Even a three year old can learn to do this. In many cases it took weeks to reunite children with surviving family members, because they only knew their first name.

B. With the churches and the community

Can a church develop a code of church bell-ringing or drum-beating? One rhythm means, "Come here for shelter." Another means, "Danger here." Talk about the simple messages that might make sense if disaster struck.

Churches should also connect with other churches for mutual support in times of need. Could you develop partnerships between rural and urban churches for emergency situations? If so, people who needed to relocate suddenly, or needed food and water, would know where to go to get help from members of another church.

How do your church plans fit in with the community plans? Who should be involved in discussing these plans?

C. With the outside world

When trouble comes to an area it is very important to have a way of making this known to the outside world. This may be done with media contacts, or by contacting those who have prayed for the people in that area, or through local NGOs, both Christian and non-Christian ones. This will help bring aid to the area.

5. How Can We Prepare Spiritually for Difficult Situations?

Many people have questions about God right now, and these questions are hard to answer. As a spiritual leader, you can guide your people through these questions, but there may be many things that even you don't understand. As you prepare for an uncertain future, it's more important to have faith than to have answers. If your people use this tragedy to turn toward God rather than away from him, they will be spiritually strengthened (Romans 5:3-5).

With that in mind, here are some ways you could prepare people to stay close to God in the next crisis.

- Do not panic in the face of danger but quickly say a short prayer.
- Memorize some Scripture passages beforehand that will help in these difficult situations.
- Cooperate with other Christians; work together for everyone's safety. Particularly protect children and the elderly.
- Recognize that there might be difficult decisions to be made, like saving one person while leaving another. God understands, and God forgives.

CLOSING EXERCISE

As we look into the future, no one can know what will happen. Even if we plan ahead, we can never be sure how we will behave in a crisis. But we do know God will be with us, even in pain and suffering. Share your hopes and fears for the future, and pray for each other and for your community.

FINAL CEREMONY

Participants will need a small piece of paper and a pen or pencil. The cross from Lesson 8 will be needed again, as well as a way to burn the papers. Participants will be comfortable participating in this ceremony because they used similar methods to bring their wounds and pain to Jesus in Lesson 8.

If possible, this final ceremony should close with a communion service.

1. Knowing God's Healing

The leader should remind the participants of the exercise "Taking Your Pain to the Cross." He or she should ask if there are other wounds that they have in their hearts that need healing. Some time should be given for silent prayer, and then the leader should pray for God's healing and blessing on everyone.

2. Opening Your Heart to God

The crisis may have brought many questions, doubts, and complaints to your heart. You may have felt angry with God, even if you weren't sure how to express that. Maybe you've been holding a grudge against God, holding back a piece of your heart because you blame him for the pain you have suffered. It's time to let that go.

Many faithful people have had questions, doubts, and complaints against God, beginning with the Bible.

- Moses, the great leader of Israel, had regular arguments with God.

- David, the sweet singer of Israel, wrote many Psalms of complaint.

- Jeremiah, the weeping prophet, questioned God's plans for his people.

- Paul, the apostle to the Gentiles, kept praying for something God wouldn't give.

- Thomas, the doubting disciple, eventually worshiped Jesus as "my Lord and my God."

- Even Jesus, facing the cross, asked his Father to change plans. And from the cross he cried, "My God, my God, why have you forsaken me?"

It is never wrong to communicate with God about your true feelings, even if those feelings are full of doubt and pain. Open your heart to him.

 EXERCISE

Read aloud the following Bible passage.

Psalms 103:8-18

The LORD is compassionate and gracious,
    slow to anger, abounding in love.
He will not always accuse,
    nor will he harbor his anger forever;
he does not treat us as our sins deserve
    or repay us according to our iniquities.
For as high as the heavens are above the earth,
    so great is his love for those who fear him;
as far as the east is from the west,
    so far has he removed our transgressions from us.
As a father has compassion on his children,
    so the LORD has compassion on those who fear him;
for he knows how we are formed,
    he remembers that we are dust.
As for man, his days are like grass,
    he flourishes like a flower of the field;
the wind blows over it and it is gone,
    and its place remembers it no more.
But from everlasting to everlasting
    the LORD'S love is with those who fear him,
    and his righteousness with their children's children—
with those who keep his covenant
    and remember to obey his precepts.

3. Repenting from Personal Sin and Knowing God's Forgiveness

Sometimes when we disagree with things God has done, we can forget about bad things that we have done. We need to acknowledge our own sin to set things right.

The leader should read the following verses aloud:

1 John 1:8-10

If we say that we have no sin, we deceive ourselves, and there is no truth in us. But if we confess our sins to God, he will keep his promise and do what is right: he will forgive us our sins and purify us from all our wrongdoing. If we say that we have not sinned, we make a liar out of God, and his word is not in us.

Isaiah 53:5-6

But because of our sins he was wounded,
    beaten because of the evil we did.
We are healed by the punishment he suffered,
    made whole by the blows he received.
All of us were like sheep that were lost,
    each of us going his own way.
But the LORD made the punishment fall on him,
    the punishment all of us deserved.

 EXERCISE

1. *Ask forgiveness for any sins you know you have committed. People take time alone to ask God to show them any sins they have not asked forgiveness for. These may have happened during the recent crisis, or just as part of ordinary life. Write these down on a piece of paper.*

2. *Know God's forgiveness for these sins. The leader says a prayer that acknowledges God's forgiveness for those who have repented. The following prayer from the Anglican prayer book could be used:*

Almighty and most merciful Father,
we have erred and strayed from your ways like lost sheep,
we have followed too much the devices and desires of our own hearts,
we have offended against your holy laws,
we have left undone those things which we ought to have done,
and we have done those things which we ought not to have done.

But you, O Lord, have mercy upon us,

spare those who confess their faults,

restore those who are penitent,

according to your promises declared to mankind

in Christ Jesus our Lord;

and grant, O most merciful Father, for his sake,

that we may hereafter live a godly, righteous, and sober life,

to the glory of thy holy Name. Amen.

4. Forgiving Others

The leader should give a brief summary of Lesson 9, reminding everyone of what forgiveness is and what forgiveness is not, and why God wants us to forgive people. Then the leader should read Romans 12:1721 aloud:

If someone has done you wrong, do not repay him with a wrong. Try to do what everyone considers to be good. Do everything possible on your part to live in peace with everybody. Never take revenge, my friends, but instead let God's anger do it. For the scripture says, "I will take revenge, I will pay back, says the Lord." Instead, as the scripture says: "If your enemies are hungry, feed them; if they are thirsty, give them a drink; for by doing this you will make them burn with shame." Do not let evil defeat you; instead, conquer evil with good.

 EXERCISE

1. *Each person should take time alone to think and pray about others they need to forgive. Write these down on a piece of paper.*

2. *Everyone returns to the group. Some people may wish to publicly forgive someone, or to confess sins against a particular ethnic group. This should not be forced, but the opportunity should be given.*

5. Bring Your Sin and the Wrongs You Haven't Forgiven to the Cross

Bring the paper on which you wrote your sin and the wrongs you just haven't been able to forgive to the cross. Nail it to the cross, or put it in the box at the foot of the cross. As you do, say, "I'm handing over my sins to Jesus who died on the cross for me."

When all the papers have been deposited, take them outside and burn them. This shows that our sins are forgiven and that we have forgiven others.

6. Final Closing Moments

It is an excellent idea to finish with a communion service where everyone together praises God for his forgiveness and for their oneness in Christ.

Recommended Readings

Amalembe, Wilfred, et. al, eds, Growing Together: A Guide for Parents and Youth, Nairobi, Kenya: MAP International, 1996.

Cloud, Henry and John Townsend, How People Grow: What the Bible Reveals about Personal Growth, Grand Rapids, MI: Zondervan Books, 2001.

Dortzbach, Debbie, AIDS in Kenya: The Church's Challenge and the Lessons Learned, Nairobi, Kenya: MAP International, 1998.

Hughes, Selwyn, How to Help a Friend, Great Britain: CWR, 1994.

___ Your Personal Encourager: Biblical Help for Dealing with Difficult Times, Great Britain: CWR, 1994.

Kilbourn, Phyllis, ed., Healing the Children of War: A Handbook for Ministry to Children Who Have Suffered Deep Traumas, Monrovia, California: MARC Publications, 1995.

Lloyd, Rhiannon and Kristine Bresser, Healing the Wounds of Ethnic Conflict: The Role of the Church in Healing, Forgiveness, and Reconciliation, Unpublished manuscript.

Sinclair, N. Duncan. Horrific Traumata: A Pastoral Response to the Post-Traumatic Stress Disorder. N.Y: Haworth Pastoral Press, 1993.

Tabifore, Henry and Sam Mulyanga, How to Teach Children Sexuality: A Handbook for Parents and Teachers, Alpha & Omega Publications, Nairobi, Kenya.

Willard, Dallas, The Divine Conspiracy: Rediscovering our Hidden Life in God, San Francisco: Harper Collins, 1998.

Both MAP International and Paulines Publications Africa have significant resources for the Church in the area of how to respond to the challenges of HIV/AIDS.

MAP International
P.O. Box 21663
00505 Nairobi, KENYA
E-mail: mapesa@map.org
Website: www.map.org

Paulines Publications Africa
Daughters of St Paul
P.O. Box 49026, 00100 Nairobi, KENYA
E-mail: publications@paulinesafrica.org
Website: www.paulinesafrica.org

HUMAN
QUESTIONS
AND GOD'S
RESPONSE

A Scripture Guide
for Church Leaders

David C Cook®

This Haitian edition is provided free to Pastors and Church Leaders by David C. Cook.
David C. Cook, 4050 Lee Vance View, Colorado Springs, CO 80918 U.S.A.
Haitian Edition: 2010

This guide is written in the hope that it will provide assistance to you who are pastors and lay leaders as you minister to those who have been touched by the January 2010 earthquake. You're dealing with hard questions from hurting people, questions for which there are no simple answers. However, this section of the Haiti Trauma Kit may help by providing some biblical principles.

Human Questions and God's Response is not meant to be an exhaustive list of questions or of Scriptures. It will, at best, provide a starting point as you care for the people around you. May the Holy Spirit use these thoughts and Scriptures to inspire you to find more Scriptures. You will want to add them in the space provided.

When you search Scripture for God's response to human questions, you'll find that people's questions fall into three primary categories:

(1) "Who is God?"

(2) "Why did this happen?"

(3) "How can I go on living?"

You may be struggling with these questions, too. God doesn't mind. In fact, he encourages us to share our true feelings and our doubts. There is so much that we cannot understand that, at some point, all answers come down to a cry to the Lord, "I believe; help my unbelief" (Mark 9:24).

May God's faithfulness and goodness become ever more evident. God's people around the world are praying for you.

1. WHO IS GOD?

Can we depend upon the trustworthiness of God's self-revelation in Scripture and in Jesus the Christ?

The verses in this section all relate to the character of God and to his faithfulness. God limits his use of his power on the earth so that we human beings might truly have free will. God doesn't intervene to stop an earthquake from injuring or killing people and destroying homes, but that in no way means that he doesn't care. Questions, however, still remain.

If God loves us, how could he allow this to happen?

> **Psalms 117:1-2:** Great is [God's] love toward us, and the faithfulness of the LORD endures forever. Praise the LORD.

I Corinthians 1:9: God, who has called you into fellowship with his Son, Jesus Christ our Lord, is faithful.

II Timothy 2:13: If we are faithless, [God] will remain faithful, for he cannot disown himself.

Psalms 62:8, 11: God is our refuge. . . .You, O God, are strong, and . . .you, O Lord, are loving.

Psalms 136:1: Give thanks to the LORD, for he is good. *His love endures forever.*

1 John 1:5: God is light; in him there is no darkness at all.

Romans 8:32, 38-39: [God] who did not spare his own Son, but gave him up for us all – how will he not also, along with him, graciously give us all things? . . . For I am convinced that neither death nor life, neither angels nor demons, neither the present nor the future, . . . nor anything else in all creation, will be able to separate us from the love of God that is in Christ Jesus our Lord.

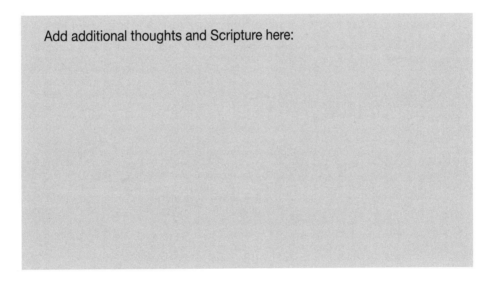

Add additional thoughts and Scripture here:

How can I believe God has not forsaken me?

Hebrews 13:5b: God has said, "Never will I leave you; never will I forsake you."

Jeremiah 29:11: "For I know the plans I have for you," declares the LORD, "plans to prosper you and not to harm you, plans to give you hope and a future."

John 3:16: For God so loved the world that he gave his one and only Son, that whoever believes in him shall not perish but have eternal life.

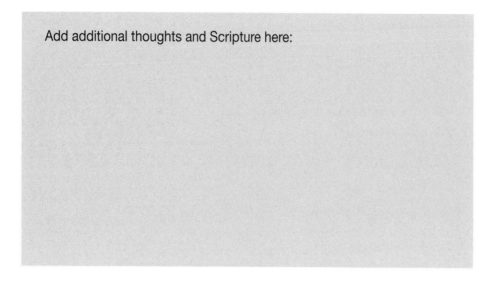

Add additional thoughts and Scripture here:

2. WHY DID THIS HAPPEN?

"Why?" questions are very difficult to answer satisfactorily. Because we are finite beings and God is infinite, we are not capable of understanding the "big picture." It's as if people are looking at the back of a piece of embroidered cloth or tapestry. The pattern and beauty of the front is not visible on the back. The back looks more like a mess of knots and threads than a picture. While God sees the completed picture of our lives, all we can see is the knotted, messy parts. It is a matter of perspective. In essence, God is God, and we are not!

In the book of Job, after Job has asked for an explanation of the disasters which have befallen him, God's response seems almost uncaring. God enumerates his many acts of creation and asks Job if Job could do any of those things. Job, of course, admits that he cannot do God's work, nor did he even observe God's creative activities. In other words, God reminds Job that God is God, and he is not, and Job is satisfied.

Although some believers think that God does not welcome such questions, there are many psalms which include questions about why certain things are happening. See, for example, Psalms 10, 22, and 88. The book of Psalms is the prayer book of the Bible. We have to conclude that God is not annoyed by hard and accusing questions but welcomes them, even though he does not always answer them as completely as we would wish.

Why did so many people die?

There is no one answer. We can point to construction that couldn't withstand an earthquake of this magnitude or lack of a plan should one hit, but the spiritual answer is that death, brought into the world by Adam and Eve's sin, is God's enemy. Death seems to be in control but death will not have the last say. God will overcome death.

I Corinthians 15:26: The last enemy to be destroyed is death.

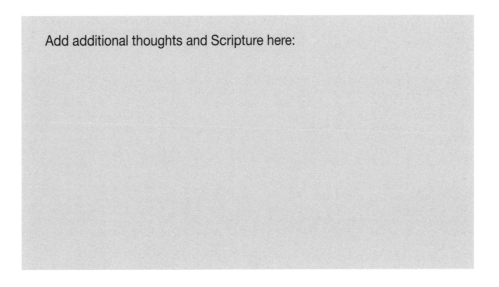

Add additional thoughts and Scripture here:

Why didn't God stop the earthquake?

Romans 8:18-25 tells us that "creation waits in eager expectation" to be freed from "its bondage to decay and brought into the glorious freedom of the children of God." Christians look forward to the time when God will make the earth perfect again, the way it was at creation before sin changed everything.

Genesis 3 and following: The entire earth was affected by the Fall of Adam and Eve.

Job 1:6-7: Satan roams through the earth, going back and forth in it.

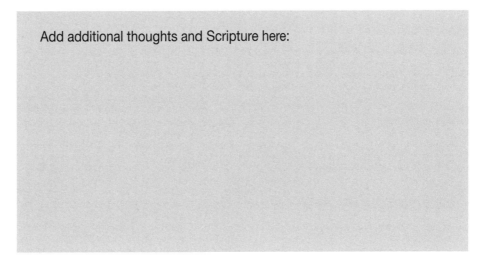

Add additional thoughts and Scripture here:

Why did God spare me?

It is possible that God has work for you to do, lessons for you to learn or share, joy for you to experience.

> **Romans 8:28:** And we know that in all things God works for the good of those who love him, who have been called according to his purpose.

> **Romans 12:15:** Rejoice with those who rejoice; mourn with those who mourn.

> **1 Corinthians 12:4-6:** There are different kinds of gifts, but the same Spirit.

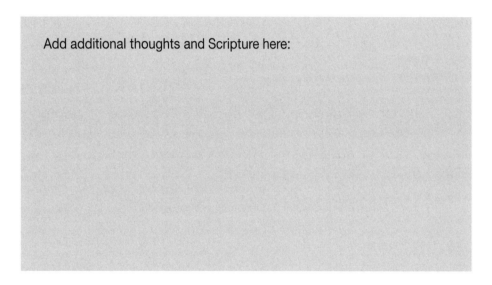

Add additional thoughts and Scripture here:

Why did this happen? Does God hate Haiti and Haitians? Haiti had already suffered so much even before the earthquake. Are we being punished for something?

The best we humans can do is to examine our own hearts and consciences, and ask that we have teachable spirits, remembering that everyone in all nations is a sinner and is dependent upon God's grace and mercy. Romans 3:10-18 reminds us that "There is no one righteous, not even one." Romans 3:23 points out that there is no difference between the people of Haiti and the people of the rest of the world. "For all have sinned and fall short of the glory of God."

Dr. Dieumeme Noelliste, Vice Chairman of the Board for the Caribbean Evangelical Theological Association in Port-au-Prince answered these questions this way: "I don't believe the country is cursed. But the terrible results of the earthquake could have been less if the Haitian society had had even a modest disaster response mechanism. Hundreds of lives could have been saved. Leadership was woefully lacking, and that includes the leadership of the church. Christian voices were silent. But today groups of Haitian Christian leaders are meeting and asking, 'What must we do? How can we use what has happened to bring material and spiritual healing to our country?'"

> **Psalm 127:1-2:** Unless the LORD builds the house, its builders labor in vain.

> **Ezekiel 18:30b-32:** I take no pleasure in the death of anyone, declares the Sovereign LORD.

> **Romans 3:19-26:** For all have sinned and fall short of the glory of God, and are justified freely by his grace through the redemption that came by Christ Jesus.

> **Matthew 5:45:** [Your Father in heaven] causes his sun to rise on the evil and the good, and sends rain on the righteous and the unrighteous.

> **John 3:16 and following:** For God did not send his Son into the world to condemn the world, but to save the world through him.

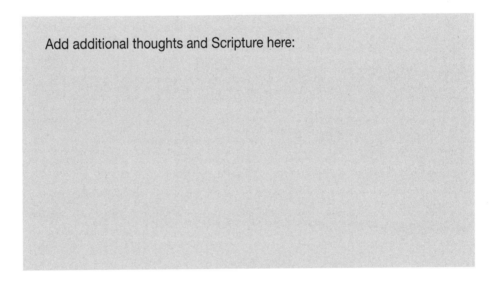

Add additional thoughts and Scripture here:

3. HOW CAN I GO ON LIVING?

"Will I ever stop crying? I cannot feel anything but sadness. I cannot even pray." These statements are full of pain.

When praying seems difficult or impossible, read or recite the Psalms as prayers instead of trying to pray yourself. All human emotions are present in the Psalms, from the most joyful elation to the darkest pit of depression and fear. God wants us to be honest in our praying. He is less concerned about the eloquence and "politeness" of our prayers than he is about how real we will be with him.

Romans 8:26-27: The Spirit helps us in our weakness. We do not know what we ought to pray, but the Spirit himself intercedes for us with groans that words cannot express.

Isaiah 25:8: He will swallow up death forever. The Sovereign LORD will wipe away the tears from all faces. (See also Revelation 7:17, 21:1-5: There will be no more death or mourning or crying or pain, for the old order of things has passed away.)

Ecclesiastes 3:1-8: There is a time for everything, and a season for every activity under heaven. . . . a time to weep and a time to laugh, a time to mourn and a time to dance.

John 11 (The death and Jesus' raising of Lazarus). The shortest verse in the Bible, John 11:35, carries deep meaning for people who mourn. " Jesus wept." He understands our sorrow.

Lamentations 3:19-26: Because of the LORD's great love we are not consumed, for his compassions never fail. They are new every morning; . . . The LORD is my portion; therefore I will wait for him.

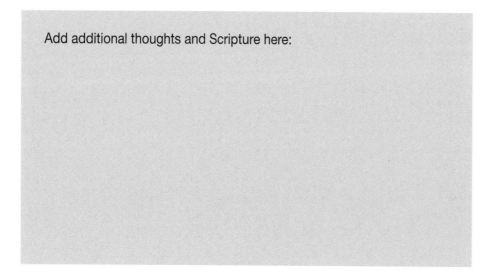

Add additional thoughts and Scripture here:

Where are my children now? What happens to children when they die?

Luke 10:21: Jesus praises the Father because he has "hidden these things from the wise and learned, and revealed them to little children."

Mark 10:13-16: Jesus said, "Let the little children come to me, and do not hinder them, for the kingdom of God belongs to such as these. . . . And he took the children in his arms, put his hands on them and blessed them.

In 2 Samuel 12:23, David is told that his son, born from his adultery with

Bathsheba, has died. His response shows that he knows he will see his son someday. "Can I bring him back again? I will go to him, but he will not return to me."

Add additional thoughts and Scripture here:

How can I go on living?

Matthew 11:28-30: [Jesus said] "Come to me, all you who are weary and burdened, and I will give you rest. . . . I am gentle and humble in heart, and you will find rest for your souls."

Isaiah 40:28-31: Have you not known? Have you not heard? The LORD . . . gives strength to the weary and increases the power of the weak. . . . Those who hope in the LORD will renew their strength. They will soar on wings like eagles; they will run and not grow weary, they will walk and not be faint."

John 15:16: I [Jesus] chose you to go and bear fruit that will last.

Psalm 23: The LORD is my shepherd. . . . He restores my soul.

2 Corinthians 4:16-18: Therefore we do not lose heart. Though outwardly we are wasting away, yet inwardly we are being renewed day by day. . . . So we fix our eyes not on what is seen, but on what is unseen.

Add additional thoughts and Scripture here:

A prayer for Christian leaders who will use this guide:

Holy Spirit, teach them and fill them so that in all they say and do, they will bring Jesus "with skin on" into the lives of hurting and questioning people. May the words of their mouths and the meditation of their hearts be pleasing in your sight, O LORD, their strong Rock and their Redeemer. Amen.

"Human Questions and God's Response" was developed for David C. Cook's Haiti Trauma Kit by Chaplain May H. Hertel, an ordained pastor and hospice chaplain.

Design and illustration: Scott Johnson, BMB Design

Haitian Creole translators: Jean Killick Aristide & Marie Nehemie Aristide

Reviewed for best practices in helping people deal with death by Janet McCormack, D.Min., B.C.C. and Heather Davediuk Gingrich, Ph. D., both at Denver Seminary, Colorado U.S.A.

Resource Expert: Dr. Dieumeme Noelliste, Vice Chairman of the Board of STEP (Seminary of Evangelical Theology of Port-au-Prince). He is professor of Theological Ethics, Denver Seminary.

David ⓒ Cook

when
you lose
someone
you love

When You Lose
Someone You Love

comfort for
those who grieve

richard exley

David C Cook®

WHEN YOU LOSE SOMEONE YOU LOVE
Published by David C. Cook
4050 Lee Vance View
Colorado Springs, CO 80918 U.S.A.
David C. Cook Distribution Canada
55 Woodslee Avenue, Paris, Ontario, Canada N3L 3E5

David C. Cook U.K., Kingsway Communications
Eastbourne, East Sussex BN23 6NT, England

David C. Cook and the graphic circle C logo
are registered trademarks of Cook Communications Ministries.

The Web site addresses recommended throughout this book are offered as a resource to you. These Web sites are not intended in any way to be or imply an endorsement on the part of David C. Cook, nor do we vouch for their content.

Editor for Haiti edition: Cynthia Bezek

Design and illustration: Scott Johnson, BMB Design

Haitian Creole translators: Jean Killick Aristide & Marie Nehemie Aristide

Reviewed for best practices in helping people deal with death by Janet McCormack, D.Min., B.C.C. and Heather Davediuk Gingrich, Ph. D., both at Denver Seminary, Colorado U.S.A.

Resource Expert: Dr. Dieumeme Noelliste, Vice Chairman of the Board of STEP (Seminary of Evangelical Theology of Port-au-Prince). The school in Port-au-Prince was destroyed in the earthquake and one student died. Dr. Noelliste is professor of Theological Ethics, Denver Seminary.

LCCN 2009907120
ISBN 978-1-4347-6480-5

© 2009 Richard Exley

First Haitian edition published in 2010.
First edition published by Honor Books in 1991
© Richard Exley, ISBN 978-1-56292-116-3

Printed in the United States of America

The book, *When You Lose Someone You Love,* is a case study built around the letters a pastor writes to Jean, a Christian man who lost his beloved wife in the earthquake. The man called Jean is actually a composite of a number of people who have lost loved ones.

As they read, pastors and church leaders will gain understanding in how to deal with the struggles grieving Christians are going through.

If possible, a leader should read this book with another person from the same church or community so that together they can talk about what they will share with real friends who are going through the trauma of losing a loved one.

ABOUT THE AUTHOR

Richard Exley has served as a pastor for 43 years. In his ministry, he often found himself praying with and counseling with hurting people who had lost loved ones. Many of these Christians were dealing with trauma that accompanies loss. They desperately needed a Christian who did not have all the answers, but did care and could walk along side them through the valley of the shadow of death.

PRAYER FOR HAITI

By Pastor Richard Exley

Have mercy upon us, O Lord. We are in desperate need of Your help. Many of us have lost everything – our homes, our livelihood and even our families. Everywhere we look we see devastation and ruin and we are tempted to despair. Comfort us in our grief, heal the wounds of our soul and restore our hope.

In the name of Jesus I pray. Amen.

NOTE TO THE READER

I wrote *When You Lose Someone You Love* while serving as the senior pastor of a local congregation. As so many leaders in Haiti today, I desperately needed a scripturally sound and practical book to give to grieving people. Not a book about grief—there were a number of those available, and not an autobiographical account of one person's grief—but a book that would speak directly to the grieving person, addressing the questions that person was dealing with as he or she walked through the valley of the shadow of death.

Having ministered to a number of grieving people during my 25 years in the pastorate, I knew how much energy it took to grieve; therefore the book had to be small. It also had to be real, honestly addressing the gut-wrenching issues death brings, especially the death of a child or the sudden and unexpected death of a spouse. And it had to be personal without being invasive, as well as scripturally sound but not preachy.

Although I found a number of excellent books, many of which are referenced in the notes and bibliography, I couldn't find exactly what I was looking for. Finally, I decided to take a stab at writing my own. I decided to make this book a series of letters addressed to a grieving person named "Jean." As you might suspect, Jean is not a real person; rather he is a composite of all the grieving people I have worked with. In order to protect their privacy, I have changed their names, and, in some instances, altered specific details regarding their loss. However, the reality of their grief and the concerns it gave birth to have been preserved as accurately as my memory affords. And because the individuals from whom this composite was constructed are real, the questions Jean raises and the issues he deals with in regard to the death of his beloved are also real.

I chose the letter style because it affords me the opportunity to speak to you directly and in a very personal manner. Although you and I have never met, I feel like I know you because we have both traveled the path of loss and grief. In some small way, I have shared your pain and therefore I feel I can speak into your life.

I have no easy answers, no glib assurances, and I won't pretend that I know what you are feeling. I may have some idea, having walked this way with others who have experienced a loss similar to your own, but that is all—just an idea. Still, it is a place to begin, and if you will allow me to speak to you from the pages of this book, I believe the Lord will comfort you. Nothing I have written will take your pain away—only God can do that—but it will help you understand what you are experiencing and how to get through it.

I won't lie to you. There will be times when the pain will be nearly more than you can bear, but God will be with you and He will sustain you. He may not take the pain away, but He will give you the strength to bear it. And as great as your grief is, God's grace is greater still.

One final thing: The Lord is no respecter of persons (Acts 10:34 KJV), and what He has done for other grieving people He will do for you. Having witnessed His grace firsthand, I can assure you that no matter how much you are suffering, God will see you through, for He is the "Father of compassion and the God of all comfort, who comforts us in all our troubles" (2 Corinthians 1:3–4).

—Richard Exley

To all those men and women who, in their grief,
taught me not only how to grieve, but also
how to find the comfort of God

Then the end will come, when [Christ] hands over the kingdom to God the Father after he has destroyed all dominion, authority and power. For he must reign until he has put all his enemies under his feet. The last enemy to be destroyed is death.

—1 Corinthians 15:24–26

When Death Comes
The first letter

Dear Jean,

How often I think of the loss of your beloved and the anguished grief to which it gave birth. The initial moments have been indelibly imprinted upon my mind. I can still see you smiling bravely as you rose to greet me when I came to give what comfort I could. Somehow that brave smile was even more heartrending than the sobs that came later. Even in the moment of your loss, you still wanted to care for me and make my task easier.

In your grief, you said that you felt handicapped, that you had never had to deal with anything like this before. How right you are. Nothing in life really prepares us for the death of a loved one, especially if that death is tragic and totally unexpected. Although we know that people—even children—die every day, we never think it can happen in our family or in our whole country.

Still, sooner or later all of us are confronted with the inevitable. It may come unexpectedly, as it did for tens of thousands of people who died in the catastrophic earthquake in Haiti on January 12, 2010. It may come less suddenly, as the result of fatal injuries or an illness. However it happens, it is always painful and inevitably followed by grief and an almost overwhelming sense of loss.

I won't pretend that I know entirely what you are feeling or that I can fully comprehend the depth of your grief. Nor will I pretend that I have all the answers to your tormenting questions. In truth, all I really have to share is my love and the painful lessons I have learned while dealing with my own grief and while helping others deal with theirs.

My first experience with death came when I was just nine years old. Mother was taken to the hospital sometime in the middle of the night, and Grandma came to stay with my two brothers and me. For the next two and a half days, Mother struggled to give birth to her fourth child. She succeeded only after the doctors belatedly performed a cesarean section. I was too young to understand any of this, but I can remember the laughter and cheers when Grandma told us that we had a baby sister. In minutes we were announcing it to the neighborhood.

Some time later, Dad came home and gathered us three boys around him. He was bowed with weariness and grief. With great difficulty, he told us the painful news. Yes, Mother had given birth to a daughter, our long-awaited sister, but things didn't look good. The baby wasn't expected to live. Even if she did live, she would never be normal and healthy.

Tears were running down Dad's cheeks when he finished, and I seemed to be smothering. I couldn't get my breath. I sat there numbly for a minute; then I burst out of the house, choking on my sobs. For the better part of the next hour, I lay facedown on the dirt. Great heaving sobs convulsed my small frame, and it seemed like everything in the universe withdrew, leaving me alone with my pain. The dust mingled with my tears, becoming mud, and I pounded my fists into the ground until I had no strength left. After a long while, my grief seemed to exhaust itself, leaving me with a hollow feeling in the pit of my stomach.

I think I accepted Johanne's death that afternoon, but it wouldn't become a reality until just before Christmas, three months later. The intervening weeks were filled with several Crisis. Once, Dad and Aunt Elsie rushed to the hospital. When they arrived, Johanne was critical, at the point of death. The doctors were able to stabilize her condition, and after she had spent several days in the hospital, they brought her home for the last time. I vaguely remember Mother placing Johanne in my lap as I sat in the armchair. She watched with a painful love as I tried to coax my baby sister to drink from a baby bottle.

It seemed that each day brought some new disappointment. Soon we realized that Johanne was both blind and deaf, and her head, larger than the rest of her tiny body at birth, became increasingly disproportionate. With a pain that still lingers, I remember watching Mother as she bathed Johanne tenderly, then carefully measured her head to see if, by some miracle, it was any smaller. It never was. Mama would bite her lip, and silent tears ran down her cheeks as she put away the cloth tape measure.

Johanne died in her sleep at home early one morning. Our family doctor and Aunt Elsie arrived at about the same time. He confirmed the death, and Aunt

Elsie fixed breakfast, which no one ate. A short time later, the mortician came and took Johanne's tiny body away, and the gray December day passed in a maze of necessary activities.

The funeral service and the trip to the cemetery have been completely blocked from my memory, leaving me without a single detail. However, I do remember eating supper after the funeral. Grief rendered the food tasteless, but we ate anyway, mechanically, out of some misbegotten sense of obligation. We ate with one small lamp as the only light. It cast deep shadows around the table, shadows that matched the sorrow in our hearts. To this day, I have not had a sadder meal.

As a child, I was able to accept Johanne's death without affixing responsibility. It was enough to know that she was with Jesus, in heaven, where there is no more sickness or pain, no more sorrow or crying. By Christmas her death was already becoming a painful but fading memory.

The questions came later, after I became a pastor and found myself ministering to families in similar situations. Their desperate questions gave birth to my own: Was God to blame for Johanne's death? Did He kill her, or at least allow her to die? Questions like these drove me to my knees. Desperately I searched the Scriptures for understanding.

After months of painful agonizing, I concluded that sin, not God, is responsible for disease, disaster, and death. That is not to say that Johanne's death was the result of her own personal sin, or even—God forbid—the sin of her parents. Rather, it means that sin has tainted the entire human race, and diseases, disasters, and death are the inevitable consequences. Romans 5:12 (KJV) declares, "Wherefore, as by one man sin entered into the world, and death by sin; and so death passed upon all men."

As I counsel those who question why humans must suffer, sometimes I simplistically explain that we inhabit a planet which is in rebellion, that we are part of a race living outside of God's will, and that one consequence of that rebellion is sickness and death. God doesn't send this plague upon people, nor does He will it. It is simply a natural consequence of humanity's fallen state. Although as believers we are new creations in Christ (2 Corinthians 5:17), we remain a part of this human family—a family that is tainted by sin and death. As a consequence, we, too, suffer the inevitable repercussions of that fallen state, even though we may be personally committed to the doing of God's will and the coming of His kingdom.

In truth, the cause of sickness, tragedy, and death is not God but the hated enemy, sin. Not necessarily our personal sin, nor a specific sin—for life and death cannot be reduced to a mathematical equation—but the fact of sin.

Jesus addressed the relationship between personal sin and death in Luke

13:1–5: "Now there were some present at that time who told Jesus about the Galileans whose blood Pilate had mixed with their sacrifices. Jesus answered, 'Do you think that these Galileans were worse sinners than all the other Galileans because they suffered this way? I tell you, no! Or those eighteen who died when the tower in Siloam fell on them—do you think they were more guilty than all the others living in Jerusalem? I tell you no!'"

Jesus does not tell us why these particular individuals died while others were allowed to live, but He does make it clear that the reason for their deaths is far more complicated than mere cause and effect.

As you well know, Jean, when death strikes unexpectedly, we long for a reason, an explanation, but often there is none. In desperation we try to make some sense out of it, but often there are simply no pat answers, no ready conclusions. In times like these we must always resist the temptation to speak where God has not spoken. Beyond the simple explanation that death comes as a result of humanity's sinful state, God has not given us any insight into the "why" of individual deaths.

In many ways, Jean, death remains a mystery, even to the Christian. Why is one child taken in infancy and not another? Why does one young mother get crushed to death in the rubble of an earthquake while another walks away without a scratch? Why is a good man stricken in the prime of life, leaving behind a wife and children, while other vicious and cruel men live to a ripe old age? Why? Why? Why? The questions are almost endless, and I must admit that I am often without answers, but of this one thing I am sure— God is not to blame! In fact, when tragedy strikes, when a loved one dies, God's heart is the first of all hearts to break!

In His comfort,
Richard

Lord Jesus, my grief is unspeakable; the pain never goes away day or night. I can't sleep. It seems I lie awake all night long. I have no appetite, no interest in food. The tastiest meal is tasteless in my mouth. All the color has gone out of my world, leaving it bleak and barren. Worst of all are the tormenting questions. Why did this happen? Why didn't You intervene? Where are You when I need You?

Yet even in the darkest night I cling to You. I trust Your love and wisdom even when I cannot understand Your ways. In my heart of hearts, I know You are too wise to ever make a mistake and too loving to ever cause one of Your own needless pain. When I weep, I choose to believe that You are weeping with me. Knowing that You share my grief gives me comfort even if it doesn't take away the pain. The promise of Your presence and the hope of eternal life give me the strength to go on. With Your help I truly believe that my mourning will one day be turned into dancing, and until that happens, I will trust You. In Your holy name I pray. Amen.

There is a time for everything, and a season for every activity under heaven: a time to be born and a time to die ... a time to weep and a time to laugh, a time to mourn and a time to dance.

—Ecclesiastes 3:1–2, 4

The Truth About Grief
The second letter

Dear Jean,

By now you undoubtedly know more about grief than you ever wanted to know. You don't necessarily understand it, but you've experienced it. You know about the desolation of a destroyed house that, not so long ago, resounded to the joyous laughter of your beloved. You know about eating alone when the two of you so often enjoyed the quiet of early morning and talked of growing old together. You told me that you are painfully reminded of your aloneness and loss each time something—a few bars of a favorite song, a visit from a friend, an old snapshot—reminds you of a shared experience. Only now you have no one with whom to share your feelings.

Following the death of his beloved wife, Davy, Sheldon Vanauken in A Severe Mercy wrote:

> Along with the emptiness which is what I mean by loss, and along with the grief—loss and grief are not the same thing—I kept wanting to tell her about it. We always told each other—that was what sharing was— and now this huge thing was happening to me, and I couldn't tell her. I sometimes thought I could bear the loss and grief if only I could tell her about it.

I remember another grieving widower telling me that the hardest thing for him to bear was when something interesting or funny happened and he would think, *I must remember to tell this to Marie.* Then he would be reminded that

Marie had passed on. At such times his grief was nearly unbearable.

Because grief is so painful, you have probably been tempted to seek not only relief, but also escape. Don't! While that reaction is not unusual, it is counterproductive. As painful as your grief is, it is not a foe to be overcome but a friend to be embraced. If you insist on thinking of your grief as an enemy, you will only delay the healing process. You may deny your grief, even repress it for a time, but you cannot escape it. One way or another, you will grieve. The only real choice you have is how and when.

Grief itself is painful but not injurious. It is a wound that brings healing in much the same way a proper surgical procedure wounds the body in order to heal it. As C. S. Lewis wrote in a letter to a dear friend whose wife had died:

> I am sure it is never sadness—a proper, straight natural response to loss—
> that does people harm, but all the other things, all the resentment, dismay,
> doubt and self-pity with which it is usually complicated.

In the final analysis, Jean, grief is a healing gift from God. Jesus said, "Blessed are those who mourn, for they will be comforted" (Matthew 5:4). That promise is fulfilled when you grieve. When you weep, God weeps with you as surely as Jesus wept with Mary following the death of her brother Lazarus. And as you share your sorrow with God, you will experience His comfort and He will bear a portion of your grief. As the prophet wrote so long ago: "Surely he took up our infirmities and carried our sorrows" (Isaiah 53:4).

There are those who teach that Christians should not grieve. They falsely reason that since our loved ones have gone to be with the Lord, we should only rejoice and not weep. Don't be misled, Jean. The Scriptures teach otherwise. The apostle Paul tells us, "Rejoice with those who rejoice; mourn with those who mourn" (Romans 12:15).

And the writer of Ecclesiastes declares,

> There is a time for everything, and
> a season for every activity under heaven …
> a time to weep and a time to laugh,
> a time to mourn and a time to dance.
>
> —Ecclesiastes 3:1, 4

Jean, now is the time for you to mourn.

Paul, the foremost apologist for the resurrection, affirms both the promise of eternal life, which gives us hope in the dark hour of our loss, and the reality of death, which makes grief mandatory. In his first letter to the believers in

Thessalonica, he encourages them to grieve but not in the same way that the world grieves. He writes:

> Brothers, we do not want you to be ignorant about those who fall asleep, or to grieve like the rest of men, who have no hope. We believe that Jesus died and rose again and so we believe that God will bring with Jesus those who have fallen asleep in him. . . . He died for us so that, whether we are awake or asleep, we may live together with him.
>
> —1 Thessalonians 4:13–14; 5:10

Jean, without God, death is an unequivocal tragedy, but seen in the light of our Lord's resurrection, it is reduced to a wound to the living. Of course, this knowledge does not eliminate your pain and loss, but it does put it into perspective. You still grieve, but not with the disconsolate grief of those who have no hope of life beyond this world.

As I write these words, I can almost see you nodding, as if you want to reassure me, but with a pained and faraway look in your eyes. It's the same look I've seen from time to time as you've hinted at a crisis of faith. You've never quite put it into words, but I believe I have sensed it. If I'm reading something into your words that isn't there, please forgive me. On the other hand, if indeed you are experiencing dark times, times when your sorrow is so deep you find yourself questioning the very existence of God (or at least His goodness), then I want to encourage you. And, if possible, I would like to walk with you through your "dark night of the soul."

You are not the first person who has found himself doubting the very things that he once held most sacred and dear. In fact, such doubt is almost inevitably a part of great grief. That doesn't make your desolation any less painful, but hopefully it does make it less frightening. You are not alone if you ever find yourself tempted to conclude that God, if He exists at all, is either cruel or incompetent. But I beg you to resist that temptation. Instead, although you may feel angry with God, cling tenaciously to the conviction that He is good and merciful, even though the pain of your present circumstance seemed to indicate otherwise. By an act of your will, please choose to believe that there is more to life than meets the eye. Take encouragement from Paul who came to grips with the fact that "for now we see through a glass, darkly" (1 Corinthians 13:12 KJV).

Quite frequently we feel ashamed of our grief, asking God why she died and you lived. Somewhere we have picked up the mistaken idea that such feelings reveal something negative about our faith. Nothing could be further from the truth. Jean, the intensity of your grief does not indict your faith. Rather, it testifies to the depth of your love and the richness of the relationship you enjoyed with your beloved.

In another sense, the honest acknowledgment of your most real feelings may very well say something about the quality of your faith—not something negative either, but something positive! It takes tremendous trust to bare your heart and soul to God when it requires you to express disappointment, doubt, shame, and fear. Somewhere we have picked up the idea that these are not the kinds of emotions a "true" Christian should have. Still, for those who are grieving, such feelings are real, and in order to work through them, they must honestly share them with God. It's their only hope. Denial is nothing more than a slow death.

Perhaps my words seem blasphemous, as if I am tempting you to commit a sacrilege. Not so! God already knows what is in your heart, so what can be gained by pretending? There is a certain risk, to be sure, in expressing your doubts and unbelief, not to mention your anger. After all, you might get stuck there. Still, it is the only way. You must trust God to help you work through your feelings.

I am encouraged when I remember that in the hour of His death Jesus experienced the same kind of haunting questions that torment us, yet without being guilty of sin (Hebrews 4:15). He, too, felt that God had forsaken Him: "And at the ninth hour Jesus cried out in a loud voice, *'Eloi, Eloi, lama sabachthani?'*—which means, 'My God, my God, why have you forsaken me?'" (Mark 15:34).

But Jesus did not allow Himself to become trapped there. Having honestly expressed His soul's deepest despair, He was able to move from that tormenting question to an affirmation of His faith: "'Father, into your hands I commit my spirit.' When he had said this, he breathed his last" (Luke 23:46).

Although His circumstances were obviously different from yours, I think there is a truth to be learned. You cannot get beyond your doubts and fears until you honestly face them in God's presence. Having done that, you are free to reaffirm your faith and recommit yourself to the God of all grace!

Of course, that doesn't mean that you are finished with your grief—but that's a letter for another day. It does, however, signal progress. You have moved into a new dimension, a new honesty in your relationship with God. Now you can walk through "the valley of the shadow of death"—not without pain, but without despair, for you do not walk alone.

In His comfort,
Richard

Lord Jesus, I love You, but I'm really questioning You right now. I don't want to feel this way, but I can't seem to help myself. You have the power of life and death, yet You refused to intervene in this horrific catastrophe that claimed tens of thousands of lives. You could have prevented the earthquake but You didn't. All of us, who have such limited power, exhausted ourselves to rescue and save victims out from under the rubble, but it feels like You, who have all power, did nothing at all. You could have spared my beloved's life, but you didn't. I'm trying to understand why You didn't do anything, but right now I can't.

To make matters worse, I was denied the customary death rituals that ordinarily bring a measure of comfort. My loved one was thrown into a mass grave with hundreds of other victims. I didn't get to have a wake for her with friends, family, and neighbors keeping vigil with me. I didn't get to plan a funeral service. There's no graveside for me to visit. These things would have given dignity to her death and brought me some small solace, but I couldn't even have those. And because everyone—every single person I know—has lost someone, my grief is rendered impersonal. Who will pity and comfort me? We're all in the throes of agony and loss. We have nothing with which to comfort one another.

Hurt is making me bitter, killing the relationship You and I once shared. I want to punish You, yet even in my anger I know You are my only hope. With one hand I push You away, while with the other hand I cling to You with all my might. With a trembling faith I lift my hurt to You, trusting that You will take it from me. Replace my anger with acceptance, I pray, and my hurt with hope. I ask not for understanding, for I know I will never understand why things happened the way they did, but for trust. Give me unconditional trust that I may rest in You no matter how grievous my loss. In Your holy name I pray. Amen.

The Tides of Grief
The third letter

Dear Jean,

In your last letter, you said that just about the time you thought things were starting to get back to "normal," you were suddenly overwhelmed with a fresh wave of grief. You went on to say that when that happened, you felt your loss as acutely as in the days immediately following your beloved's death. Then you asked, "When will this terrible pain end?"

I wish I knew, but I don't. Grieving is a lengthy process and often requires two or three years to complete its healing work. Of course, you will not always grieve with the same intensity; no one could bear that. Gradually you will find that the awful edge of your grief is lessening. You will experience a renewed interest in life. It won't happen all at once, and there will be numerous reversals when you are caught once again in the painful throes of mourning. Still, as the seasons pass, you will experience a spring time in your life as the long winter of your grief draws to a close. One of the best ways to understand what is happening is found in the analogy you used, "a fresh wave of grief."

In truth, grieving is a lot like the tide; it comes in waves. Immediately following the death of a loved one, we are overwhelmed with a sense of loss and the accompanying sadness. The tide of grief comes rushing in, but we are protected from the enormity of our loss by shock, by the details surrounding the death, and by the comforting presence of family and friends. However, once the first shock ends and we get caught up in new routines, we experience a great weariness and an unspeakable sadness.

Although this is an overwhelmingly difficult time, it is not unexpected. You were prepared for it; that is, as much as anyone can prepare for something like this. With determination you suffered through those first few weeks. There were moments of fear, moments when you were incensed by the injustice of it all, and moments when you were tempted to blame God. At other times I know you were unbearably sad. There were even periods of depression when you were tempted to isolate yourself. Still, little by little the awful edge of your grief dulled. Then, you said, you still hurt, but it was less a searing pain and more a stubborn ache.

Then came the day, at last, when you seemed to awaken from the long night of your grief. It would be going too far to say that you were happy, but at least you were not unhappy, not sad.

For the first time since that fateful moment when the ground shook and everything tumbled around you, you felt like your old self. You concluded, incorrectly, that you were over your grief. In truth, what you were experiencing that day is similar to what people who are sick feel when they finally turn the corner following a lengthy illness. The sky suddenly seems bluer, the sun brighter, and a zest for living returns, but there will still be many days of recuperation before they fully recover.

In *A Grief Observed,* C. S. Lewis says,

> There are moments, most unexpectedly, when something inside me tries to assure me that I don't really mind so much, not so very much, after all. Love is not the whole of a man's life. I was happy before I ever met H. I've plenty of what are called "resources." People get over these things. Come, I shan't do so badly.... Then comes a sudden jab of red-hot memory and all this "commonsense" vanishes like an ant in the mouth of a furnace.

I believe that pretty well sums up what is happening to you. Following a brief period when you seemed relatively free of grief, you suddenly find yourself grieving again. To use your analogy, when you finally thought you were beginning to regain your emotional equilibrium, you were blindsided by a fresh wave of grief.

Now, once again, you find yourself weeping at the oddest moments. Your melancholy has returned and you've lost all interest in life. People weary you, and yet you cannot bear the thought of being alone. You find it difficult to follow or respond to their casual conversation; it seems so uninteresting. Nevertheless, you want people around, if only they would talk to each other and not you.

This is a pattern that will repeat itself again and again over the next several months. The tides of grief will come in and go out. You will experience times of intense grief followed by periods of relative calm. Then the tide will come in again, and once more you will grieve. Just as suddenly, the tide will go out again so that, if you did not know better, you would think you were finally over your grief. Of course, you're not. This is just another "resting period" before you resume your "grief work."

As grief does its healing work, you will begin to notice some subtle changes. When the tide of grief rolls in, it will not come in quite as far, nor will it stay as long. And when it rolls back, it will go out further and stay out longer. Your times of grief will become briefer and less intense, while your times of rest will become longer and more renewing.

Another subtle change is in the way you think about your beloved. In the initial stages of grief, almost all of your thoughts are filled with loss. As you well know, you cannot think of your beloved without thinking about the horrible way she died. The trip to the mass gravesite is still a haunting memory. You brood about what might have been or what should have been. No memory of her is free from pain.

By and by, those painful memories will be replaced by earlier ones when you shared the joy of life, reminiscences of happier times when death seemed nothing more than a distant possibility. But the first few times you remember her without experiencing grief's familiar pangs, you will undoubtedly feel guilty, as if you have betrayed her memory. You may find it helpful to remember that as it is unhealthy to repress grief when you experience it. It is also unhealthy to manufacture sorrow when it is not there. Those who grieve in a healthy manner accept their feelings as valid, whether sorrow or comfort, and offer them to God in worship.

Another reason you may long to hold onto your sorrow is because it may seem to be all you have left of the life you shared together. In the book *Song for Sarah* by Paula D'Arcy, a grieving mother says,

> My feelings are the only thing I have left which hasn't been wrested from me. My tears and my pain over you are all I still have. Everything else is gone. So even if it does hurt, it's the last thing I have which is ours. These tears are all that's left of us.

In truth, the redemptive work of grief is intended to heal your broken heart so you can remember your beloved without always reliving the pain of her death. Her death may be your last memory of her, but it is not the only thing. You also shared her life, and I want to encourage you to allow the God of all comfort to balance those last painful memories with the early joyous ones. I'm not suggesting that you attempt to block out the memory of her death, but only that you make it a part of the integrated whole. As difficult as it may be, you must remember the life she lived and the times you had together.

In His comfort,
Richard

Lord Jesus, I want to thank You for never leaving me alone in my grief. Without the strength of Your presence, I don't think I could have made it. Now that my terrible pain is easing a little, I realize that You were with me even when I was sure You were nowhere to be found. I want to thank You for allowing me to vent, to honestly express my feelings, even the ones I wish I didn't have. Thank You for being patient with me, for giving me time to work through my feelings. Today is a "good" day and for that I give You thanks. A day like this makes me believe that there may even be life after my beloved's death; no matter how much I miss her or how deeply I grieve. I give You praise this day and every day. In Your holy name I pray. Amen.

When you pass through the waters, I will be with you; and when you
pass through the rivers, they will not sweep over you.
When you walk through the fire, you will not be burned;
the flames will not set you ablaze. For I am the LORD,
your God, the Holy one of Israel, your savior.

—Isaiah 43:2–3

The Pitfalls of Grief
The fourth letter

Dear Jean,

As you well know, grief is an inevitable part of our human condition. Sooner or later all of us experience the death of someone we love, and with it, the pain of grief. Yet for all of grief's familiarity, few of us are really prepared for it. As a consequence, we risk not only our future happiness, but also our emotional wholeness.

During the grieving process you must avoid two temptations, either of which can be emotionally crippling. The first is the temptation to pretend that you are fully recovered when you're not. While it is natural to hide your grief and this may seem to work for a time, in actuality, it only delays the healing process.

The second temptation is to wallow in your grief. I'm not suggesting that you deny the reality of your loss in order to appear recovered, but I know that grief has a fatal fascination for most of us. There is something "tragic," even "romantic," about those who have suffered a great loss, especially if they seem to suffer nobly. If we are not careful, "bearing our grief" can become a pseudo badge of courage. After a time it is easier to play the part of the grieving spouse or parent or child than it is to come to grips with our loss and get on with the business of living.

The most common way this second temptation manifests itself is through an abnormal and unhealthy preoccupation with grief. While it is normal to be consumed with our loss in the initial stages of grief, past a certain point it becomes counterproductive. Healthy grief may require months (even as much as two years or more) to complete its work, but it is not static. It moves from a sense of loss to one of grateful appreciation. That is to say, as grief does its healing work, the way we think about the departed will change.

Initially, all we can remember is the tragedy and our beloved's death, but after a while we begin to recall the life we shared together. This change doesn't come about all at once, nor is it final. Little by little we find ourselves remembering the good times we experienced with one another. These positive memories will be interspersed with painful episodes when the memory of their death returns with frightening clarity. Still, as time goes on, more and more of our thoughts will be of the life they lived rather than the death they died. That's the healing power of grief.

Although grief's work cannot be hurried, there are certain things we can do to facilitate it. Let me illustrate. Some years ago I was working with a mother who was mourning the accidental death of her 16-year-old son. When she came to see me, several months had passed, but the full impact of his death was just beginning to sink in. All she could think about was what he had missed. He never finished school. He would never marry or have children of his own. Her list was endless, and in great sorrow she poured out the agony of her soul.

After several sessions, I felt that the time had come for us to move on, so I gently suggested that she spend some time each day remembering the good times she had shared with her son. In order to make the memories specific, I asked her to put them in the form of a letter to her departed son. Finally, I asked her to conclude each letter with a prayer.

My purpose was really very simple. By asking her to remember the good times they had shared, I was encouraging her to recall not just her son's death, but his life as well. Of course, this did not nullify his tragic death, but it did serve to put it into the context of the life he had lived. As long as she had those special memories, her son would never be far from her thoughts. And by asking her to conclude each letter with a prayer, I was making it possible for her to give to God both her grief and her gratitude.

A few days later she wrote:

Dear Son,

Today is such a beautiful day. The sun is shining and the leaves are blowing under the trees.

Remember that day when you were little and we went to a place in the country that had big rocks? You climbed all over and said, "Look, Mom, I am king of the mountain." When it was time to go I said, "Come on, Little King," and the boys next to you said, "Little King? What a funny name for a kid." We laughed all the way home.

You were four years old then and I guess that was the day you got your nickname. You never seemed to mind that I called you Little King all these years. I love you very much.

Always,
Mom

She concluded with a prayer:

Dear God!

Thank You for the sun and the trees. Thank You for the laughter that only children can bring in their special way. Please, Lord, help me to heal my heart and spirit so I can be a light for You.

As the weeks went by, she began to recover. Little by little her good days began to outnumber her bad days. Eventually her memories of her beloved son became a source of comfort rather than searing pangs of grief. Now when she thinks of him, her first thoughts are usually of some childhood prank or of some tender, poignant moment, rather than of his fatal accident. Of course, there will always be those times—his birthday or the anniversary of his death—when she will experience again the pain of her loss. But for the most part she is now able to thank God for the 16 years she and her son had together, rather than blaming God for his premature death.

Jean, I shared all of this with you because it may be time for you to take control of your grief. For the most part it has been controlling you these past few months—and that's okay. But if you hope to get beyond this point, you will have to take some responsibility for your recovery. Maybe the time has come for you to change your focus. Heretofore you have mourned your loss. Perhaps now it is time for you to give thanks for the years you and your beloved had together, thanks for the richness of the life you shared.

A Baptist minister named John Claypool wrote a book titled *Tracks of a Fellow Struggler* in which he discusses his struggle to make some sense out of the death of his ten-year-old daughter. He concludes:

I have two alternatives: dwelling on the fact that she has been taken away, I can dissolve in remorse that all of this is gone forever, or, focusing on the wonder that she was given to us at all, I can learn to be grateful that we shared life, even for an all-too-short ten years. The way of remorse does not alter the stark reality one whit and only makes matters worse. The way of gratitude does not alleviate the pain, but it somehow puts some light around the darkness and builds strength to begin to move on.

Jean, your beloved was a gift from God, pure and simple. She was never really yours, not in the sense that we tend to think. You were privileged to enjoy life with her for a time, and now she is gone. You can hold that fact against God and grow bitter, or you can thank God you were given the gift of her presence for a time, however short.

If you choose to thank God for what you had, rather than continue to focus on what you have lost, I believe you will discover a new dimension of life. That doesn't mean you won't grieve or that you won't miss her. Rather, it means that not even death can rob you of the joys you shared together! Nor can it steal your present hope or the promise of the future. The God who makes all things new is now present to renew your life. He wants to give you the grace to enjoy living again!

In His comfort,
Richard

Lord Jesus, replace my grief with gratefulness. Help me to remember the life we shared rather than just the death she died. Replace the painful memories of her suffering with the joyous memories of our life together. Help me to remember the first time I saw her and the way she smiled at me. Let me remember our wedding day, the births of our children, and the many times we prayed together, lifting our concerns to You with thanksgiving. Let me remember her zest for living, her devotion to our family and friends, and most of all her remarkable faith. These are gifts not even death can take from me. In Your holy name I pray. Amen.

*I took you from the ends of the earth, from its farthest corners
I called you. I said, "You are my servant";
I have chosen you and have not rejected you.
So do not fear, for I am with you; Do not be dismayed,
for I am your God. I will strengthen you and help you;
I will uphold you with my righteous right hand....
For I am the LORD, your God, who takes hold of your right hand
and says to you, Do not fear; I will help you.*

—Isaiah 41:9–10, 13

The Promise
of His Presence
The fifth letter

Dear Jean,

As a minister, I have often shared the grief of those whom the Lord has entrusted to my care. Although that has been a tragically sad responsibility at times, it has also afforded me the opportunity to witness not only the faithfulness of God, but also the faith of His people and the strength faith provides, especially in the hour of our greatest loss.

Not even those who have great faith, however, endure grief without questions. Inevitably their concerns have a common theme. Although each person expresses his apprehension in his own unique way, it can generally be summed up in two or three common questions.

First, the bereaved want to know if God has forsaken them, if He has abandoned them in the dark hour of their grief. The emptiness they experience and the desolation they feel often make it seem that He has. Second, they want to be assured that God knows what they are experiencing and that He cares. Finally, they ask, "Can God bring something good out of this terrible experience?"

As you well know, Jean, one of the things that makes the death of a loved one so difficult is that we often feel that God has forsaken us. Of course, He hasn't, but there are times when it feels as if He has. Such feelings are common to those who grieve, and there is no reason to be ashamed of them. Even C. S. Lewis, the great Christian thinker and writer, struggled with feelings of abandonment following his wife's death. He wrote about that experience in *A Grief Observed:*

> Meanwhile, where is God? This is one of the most disquieting symptoms. When you are happy, so happy that you have no sense of needing Him, so happy that you are tempted to feel His claims upon you as an interruption, if you remember yourself and turn to Him with gratitude and praise, you will be—or so it feels—welcomed with open arms. But go to Him when your need is desperate, when all other help is vain, and what do you find? A door slammed in your face, and a sound of bolting and double bolting on the inside. After that, silence. You may as well turn away. The longer you wait, the more emphatic the silence will become. There are no lights in the windows. It might be an empty house. Was it ever inhabited? It seemed so once. And that seeming was as strong as this. What can this mean? Why is He so present a commander in our time of prosperity and so very absent a help in time of trouble?

In times like that, we must remember that while our feelings are real, they are not necessarily accurate. That is to say, it truly feels as if God has deserted us, that He has left us alone with our grief. He hasn't, but it feels as though He has. Through the centuries, spiritual pilgrims have referred to this sense of abandonment as "the dark night of the soul." They triumphed in those dark times by choosing to trust in the truth of God's Word rather than the raging of their emotions.

The Scriptures contain many promises of His abiding presence. Promises like Deuteronomy 31:8 declare, "The LORD himself goes before you and will be with you; he will never leave you nor forsake you. Do not be afraid; do not be discouraged."

The last thing Jesus did before ascending into heaven was to give His disciples the promise of His presence. "And surely I am with you always, to the very end of the age" (Matthew 28:20).

These promises and countless others like them are a source of tremendous strength when you are grieving. Yet, what has helped me the most in my hour of desolation is a passage from Isaiah 49:

> For the LORD comforts his people and will have compassion on his afflicted ones.

But Zion said, "The LORD has forsaken me, the Lord has forgotten me."

"Can a mother forget the baby at her breast and have no compassion on the child she has borne? Though she may forget, I will not forget you!

"See, I have engraved you on the palms of my hands."

—Isaiah 49:13–16

Can a mother forget the child she has conceived? Can she forget that joyous moment when she first felt that new life move within her womb? Can she forget the hours she spent praying and dreaming about their life together? Can she forget the moment of birth, when she went to the very doorway of death to bring forth life, when at last the awful agony of labor was forgotten in the delirious joy of holding her tiny child for the very first time? Can she forget the infant that nursed at her breast? Can she forget?

I cannot imagine how she could, but God says, "Though she may forget, I will not forget you!" In other words, the only thing worthy to be compared with God's love for us is a mother's love for her child. Yet, even that special love pales in comparison with God's eternal and unconditional love for His children. As unimaginable as it may seem, there are mothers who abandon their own children, but God will never forsake one of His own!

In the hour of grief—no, I should say in the weeks and months of grief—when it seems there will never be an end to our grieving, when it seems all of life is one sad song, we still have a choice. We can choose to believe what seems to be the truth—God is absent. Or we can ignore the visible evidence in favor of the invisible reality. We can choose to believe that God is present and that one day soon our shaken emotions will once again recognize His nearness.

Many times the pain of our loss blinds us to the reality of God's presence. Only later when we look back and review the days of our grief do we realize that He was with us all the time, even when we were sure He was nowhere to be found.

Isn't this what happened to the grieving disciples on the road to Emmaus? Jesus spent an entire day with them, even expounded the Scriptures to them, and yet they did not recognize Him. Only later, when He had disappeared from their sight, did they begin to reflect on their experience. Then they said, "Were not our hearts burning within us while he talked with us on the road and opened the Scriptures to us?" (Luke 24:32).

At other times God manifests His presence indirectly, through other people. Paul writes, "When we came into Macedonia, this body of ours had no rest, but we were harassed at every turn—conflicts on the outside, fears within. But God, who comforts the downcast, comforted us *by the coming of Titus"* (2 Corinthians

7:5–6, emphasis added).

Remember the lady I wrote about whose teenaged son died in a tragic accident? One morning when she was feeling particularly low someone knocked at her door. She wrestled momentarily with the idea of ignoring it. Her eyes were red from crying, her hair was a mess, and she hadn't gotten dressed yet. But the knocking persisted so she forced herself toward the door.

The caller was a friend from church, and when Joyce opened the door, the friend breezed right in, announcing, "I've come to talk with you." Noticing Gaelle's disheveled appearance, she quickly added, "And if you don't feel like talking, I'll just sit with you, and if you want to cry," she continued, "I'll cry with you."

By this time the uninvited guest was starting to make coffee. The two friends spent the rest of the morning over coffee laced with conversation and tears. As they talked, the strangest thing happened—Gaelle began to feel better. She was still sad, but now she was no longer alone with her sadness. A friend was present and shared her sorrow. And in some mysterious way God was present too, and He comforted her.

Think for a moment, Jean. How many times over these past weeks and months has someone been there for you? Oh, I know the many times people have failed you, perhaps because they are dealing with their own grief. You've spent long evenings alone and eaten many meals by yourself. Still, think of the times you have been comforted in your grief by a surprise visit from a neighbor or a friend who reached out to you and said just the right thing at just the right time. Coincidence? Hardly.

Remember, Jean, the hand that brings you comfort and encouragement is always God's hand, and He is never far from His own.

In His comfort,
Richard

Lord Jesus, forgive me. I have been so consumed with my grief that I have been blind to all the ways You have come to me—in the presence of my pastor, a visit from a dear friend, an invitation to join neighbors for a meal, and in the laughter of my grandchildren. At the time these things seemed no more than ordinary events, but I now realize that You were present in each and every one, bringing me comfort in that moment and hope for the future. Truly it is Your hand that comforts and encourages me. Help me to remember that You are never far from me no matter how alone I feel. In Your holy name I pray. Amen.

I have told you these things, so that in me you may have peace.
In this world you will have trouble. But take heart!
I have overcome the world.

—John 16:33

The Depth of His Love
The sixth letter

Dear Jean,

Again and again these past weeks you have asked, "Does God know what's happening to me? Does He see what has happened to Haiti? Does He care?" At other times you have wondered, "Why didn't He do something to prevent this awful tragedy?"

I've given considerable thought to your questions, and I am convinced that it's not really answers you seek as much as assurance. Intuitively you know that suffering and death are often shrouded in mystery, that there are simply no pat answers. Still, the nagging questions remain, replayed in your mind, over and over again. You long for some word, some explanation, that will restore your confidence. As it is, you are beset by a haunting uncertainty. Although you may never have put it into words, I sense that deep down you wonder if you can really trust God.

Don't be embarrassed: Your doubts are as old as mankind. In the midst of grief almost everyone is tempted to feel the way you do. Yet, at the same time you love God more intensely than you ever have. These feelings may seem contradictory to you, and you may even be tempted to wonder if you are losing your mind. You're not! Grief gives birth to a host of different emotions. The Lord understands this, and He comes to us in the midst of our emotional storms.

Following the unexpected death of their brother, Lazarus, Martha and Mary experienced an overwhelming grief, which gave birth to questions not unlike your own. Like you, they were troubled by the tragedy of losing a loved one, and they could not help but question our Lord's goodness.

"'Lord,' Martha said to Jesus, 'if you had been here, my brother would not have died'" (John 11:21). With those words she accused Jesus of failing, of not caring, of ignoring them in the hour of their greatest need. Does that sound familiar?

What did Jesus do? How did He respond? He absorbed her great disappointment without rebuke. He understood how things must seem from her limited perspective, how much she loved her brother, and how deeply she hurt.

Yet, she didn't stop there. Like you, she still loved Jesus intensely and wanted to believe. Even in her anger, her faith expressed itself: "I know he will rise again in the resurrection at the last day. . . . I believe that you are the Christ, the Son of God, who was to come into the world" (John 11:24, 27).

When she quickly moved from anger and accusation to faith, Jesus met her there and built on her confession. He said to her, "'I am the resurrection and the life. He who believes in me will live, even though he dies; and whoever lives and believes in me will never die. Do you believe this?' 'Yes, Lord,' she told him" (John 11:25–27).

Mary responded differently. She, too, was hurt and angry, maybe more hurt and angry in keeping with her temperament:

> When Mary reached the place where Jesus was and saw him, she fell at his feet and said, "Lord, if you had been here, my brother would not have died." When Jesus saw her weeping . . . he was deeply moved in spirit and troubled. . . . [And] Jesus wept" (John 11:32–33, 35).

Notice that Jesus also met Mary where she was. And there was little or no faith in her confession beyond the faith to tell Jesus how she really felt. Somehow, even in her grief and disappointment, she believed He would understand, and He did. For her, He had no theological pronouncements, no revelation about resurrection life, no discourse about His divine sonship. Why? Not because these things were any less true then, but because Mary was not ready to receive them. There was nothing in her heart but sorrow and tears, so He met her at the place of her grief. He wept with her.

If Jesus came to Martha and Mary in the hour of their grief, will He not come to you? If He understood what they were feeling and shared their feelings, will He not do as much for you? How did I put it in my first letter? "When tragedy strikes, when a loved one dies, God's heart is the first of all hearts to break!"

I'm hesitant, Jean, to give you too many Scriptures because I know that the shock of grief can render the eternal Scriptures temporarily unreal. Yet, I also know that nothing comforts and illuminates like the Word of God, especially when it is spoken in season. Nothing so quiets the frightened heart, so stills the troubled soul, as the Holy Scriptures.

Think for a moment. Haven't there been times, especially of late, when the Scriptures have spoken to the deepest and most profound longings of your soul? Haven't you discovered new words of hope and encouragement in familiar verses, passages that you've known for years? Is this mere chance? Not on your life! It is God's way of manifesting Himself, His way of comforting you in the depths of your grief.

Your questions may still remain, but somehow they don't seem quite so important now. God has given you something better than understanding—trust, a trust that is rooted not in explanation but in the assurance that He cares.

A seminary president tells of a friend who lost his daughter in a flash flood in the book, The Jesus Model, by Jean L. McKenna. He says:

> When I met him two weeks after the tragedy, his eyes were sunk in dark sockets from weeping. Awkwardly, I asked, "How is it going?"

> Never given to public testimony or eloquent statements, his sad eyes looked back, and he spoke almost from a trance, "The hurt goes deep, but His love goes deeper."

That, Jean, is the essence of trust. No matter how deep your grief, God's love goes deeper still.

In His comfort,
Richard

Lord Jesus, thank You for absorbing my raging emotions, my angry accusations, and my explosive grief without rebuke. Had I not been able to express my honest feelings to You, they would have surely poisoned my spirit. Help me not to get stuck here. Help me to work through these turbulent emotions, to move from hurt and confusion to acceptance and finally to unconditional trust. Help me to rest in Your love and in the great promises of Scripture. In Your holy name I pray. Amen.

And we know that in all things God works for the good of those who love him, who have been called according to his purpose. . . .
What, then, shall we say in response to this?
If God is for us, who can be against us?

—Romans 8:28, 31

If God Is for Us
The seventh letter

Dear Jean,

I couldn't agree with you more when you say that one of the things that makes death so difficult to accept is that it seems such a waste. As rational creatures, we find simply unbearable the thought that the ending of lives might be pointless, of no eternal value. On the other hand, if we can be assured that God will ultimately bring good out of what looks for like a senseless tragedy, then we can somehow endure it.

Given that hope, it is not uncommon for the bereaved to try to figure out how God is going to bring good out of their tragedy. It is a futile exercise for the most part, because God's ways are far beyond anything we could ever imagine. In fact, trying to discover His ultimate purpose while you are in the midst of grief often leads to absurd conclusions or to outright despair. Nevertheless, you may be assured that one day you will understand how God redeemed your terrible loss and caused it to work for eternal good.

I am not suggesting, not even for a moment, that God caused the death of your beloved, for He did not! In time you will come to see how He has turned what now seems nothing more than a senseless tragedy into a miracle of grace. The very thing that the Enemy intended to use to destroy your faith can become an instrument by which God furthers His eternal purpose in your life and in the kingdom. Just how He will do that, I don't know; but that He will do so, I am sure.

Many years ago, I heard about a minister whose son committed suicide. Ten days after the funeral, the minister stood at the pulpit and announced his text. Under real duress, he read Romans 8:28: "And we know that in all things God works for the good of those who love him, who have been called according to his purpose." Visibly struggling, he said:

> I cannot make my son's suicide fit into this passage. It's impossible for me to see how anything good can come out of it. Yet, I realize that I only see in part; I only know in part. The scope of this verse is beyond me; I can't comprehend it. Still, somehow it supports me, enables me to go on living even though life doesn't seem to make any sense. Somehow I believe that when all of life is over, when God has fully worked out His perfect will, even my son's suicide will be woven into the final tapestry of His eternal design.

It's like the miracle of the shipyard. Almost every part of our great oceangoing vessels is made of steel. If you take any single part—be it a steel plate out of the hull or the huge rudder—and throw it into the ocean, it will sink. Steel doesn't float! But when the shipbuilders are finished, when the last plate has been riveted in place, when the last part has been bolted properly, then that massive ship is virtually unsinkable. By the design of the master shipbuilder, steel has been made to float!

Taken by itself, a son's suicide is senseless. Throw it into the sea of Romans 8:28, and it sinks. But when the Eternal Shipbuilder has finally finished, when God has worked out His perfect design, even this senseless tragedy will somehow work to our eternal good. Even if we can't imagine how, know that it will!

Jean, you asked me what good can possibly come out of your beloved's death. I wish I could tell you, but I can't. All I can do is assure you that God is too wise ever to make a mistake. And He is too loving to ever allow one of His children to go through needless pain.

I see you struggling to make some sense of this tragic death, trying to see how God can possibly take a death the earthquake caused and fit it into His plan. I don't fault you for this, but I must counsel you to be careful. Death is not a riddle to be solved or a question to be answered; instead, it is a mystery to be entrusted to the wisdom of God.

Rather than trying to understand how God is going to bring good out of your beloved's death, it might be more beneficial to consider some historic examples of how He has redeemed other seemingly senseless tragedies. Quite frequently the good that God works can only be seen in retrospect. Even then we only see in part. We must wait until eternity to understand the full scope of His eternal craftsmanship.

On January 8, 1956, Jim Elliot and four other missionaries were brutally murdered by the Aucas, a savage tribe of man hunters living in the Ecuadorian jungles. At first glance, their deaths seemed like a tragic waste of life, especially Jim Elliot's. Not only was he a young husband and father, he was also a missionary of rare and special ability. Even as a college student, he had shown a remarkable spiritual maturity. His personal pilgrimage is chronicled in his diary (published posthumously as *The Journal of Jim Elliot*), which contains some of the most profound spiritual concepts recorded in the last century. His entire life was characterized by a burning passion to reach the unreached peoples of the world with the gospel of Jesus Christ. Just prior to his death, he completed a translation of the Gospel of Luke for the Quechuas, a tribe of South American Indians.

In light of all of this, we are tempted to ask why God would allow such a gifted and dedicated young man to be martyred at the age of 29. His ministry was just beginning. Surely the kingdom could not afford the loss of one so able.

Upon further examination, however, we can see God working to redeem this tragedy. When news of the deaths of the five missionaries was announced in Christian schools, hundreds of young people volunteered to take their places. The story caused world missions to be front-page news in magazines and newspapers around the world.

Helen Roseveare, who served for many years in the Belgian Congo as a missionary doctor with the Worldwide Evangelism Crusade, shared a touching incident that further shows how God brings good out of tragedy. She reports in "The Spirit's Enablement":

> A young missionary couple during their first term of service in a foreign land were expecting their first baby. The mother wrote me from the hospital a few days after the birth to tell me that her baby had died. She went on in her letter, "Local women whom I've been trying to reach with the gospel visited me yesterday, and their loving sympathy was very touching. Then one of them said to me, 'Now you are the same as us. Now we will listen to what you tell us.' I find my heart rising above my sorrow.... I can identify with the local community in their daily sufferings and so be able to share Christ with them."

Given these examples and many others like them, one might be tempted to conclude that God caused these deaths in order to advance the work of the Gospel. I cannot believe that. God is not the author of death, but of life.

Death is the archenemy of God, a consequence of humanity's fallen state. It is a defeated enemy, to be sure, but it has not yet been destroyed:

For he [Jesus] must reign until he has put all his enemies under his feet. The last enemy to be destroyed is death. . . . Then the saying that is written will come true: "Death has been swallowed up in victory."

"Where, O death, is your victory?

Where, O death, is your sting?" The sting of death is sin.... But thanks be to God! He gives us the victory through our Lord Jesus Christ.

—1 Corinthians 15:25–26, 54–57.

God uses death in the same way an expert in self-defense uses his opponent's weight and momentum against him. When death strikes, God takes that unspeakable loss and uses it as an opportunity to bring good out of evil.

Of course, Jean, I must admit that it is much easier for me to write about these truths than it is for you to live them. Although my heart hurts, my suffering is nothing compared to your grief. I can view these tragic events somewhat objectively; you cannot. In many ways I am an outside observer, while you and your fellow Haitian sufferers are the central participants. As a main participant, you obviously know more about the devastation of death; but as a more objective observer, I probably have a better understanding of the big picture. And in order to make some sense of your loss, you must not insist on seeing it as an entity unique unto itself. You must come to the place where you can view it as a single piece of an integrated whole—a piece that finds its true meaning only in relationship to the eternal whole.

In the overwhelming pain of grief, we are able to see only part of the picture, and as a result, death often seems like the ultimate insult. It appears to be the final indignity that makes a mockery of our faith. But when the fog of grief begins to clear even just a little—when at last we are able to perceive the whole truth—it becomes obvious that death is a defeated enemy, one that God uses for His eternal purposes until He ultimately destroys it:

Therefore we do not lose heart. Though outwardly we are wasting away, yet inwardly we are being renewed day by day. For our light and momentary troubles are achieving for us an eternal glory that far outweighs them all. So we fix our eyes not on what is seen, but on what is unseen. For what is seen is temporary, but what is unseen is eternal.

—2 Corinthians 4:16–18.

Jean, in closing let me say that I am not naive enough to think that anything I write can eliminate the painfulness of your grief. You do not lose someone you love dearly without experiencing the deepest sorrow of which the human heart is capable. I do believe, however, that the spiritual and emotional devastation caused by your grief can be minimized—no, more than that, redeemed—if you can be helped to see it in its eternal context. Once you have accomplished that feat, your grief will not necessarily be less, but it will become pain with a purpose. And history has shown us that humans can bear an almost unlimited amount of suffering if they can be assured that it will count for something.

Let me encourage you to offer your beloved's death, along with your grief and loss, as a gift to God. Give Him permission to use it any way He sees fit. Do this, and I truly believe that God will redeem it for His glory and your good.

In His comfort,
Richard

Lord Jesus, I know that my beloved did not live in vain. Her life was rich with meaning, and she enriched everyone whose life she touched. I'm tempted to think of her death as a waste, an unspeakable loss, but by an act of my will I choose not to. Instead I choose to remember that You have a long history of bringing good out of the most unspeakable loss. Although I cannot imagine how, I choose to believe that You will bring eternal good out of this terrible tragedy. With a trembling heart I offer you a sacrifice of praise, lifting both my beloved's death and my painful grief to You in worship. Redeem her death and my grief. In Your holy name I pray. Amen.

In My Father's House
The eighth letter

Dear Jean,

As I look back over the correspondence we have shared these past months, I am struck by the fact that we have said so little about your beloved. Our letters have focused on what has been happening to you—your grief and your loss. To an uninitiated observer this might appear self-centered, even unfeeling, but it is neither. In truth, it is an affirmation of our belief in eternal life. We have not concerned ourselves with her present state because we are confident, as Paul says, that to be absent from the body is to be present with the Lord (2 Corinthians 5:8 KJV).

Having said that, however, I do think the time has come for us to address the question of life after death. This single issue, more than any other, distinguishes the way believers grieve from the way those without the hope of eternal life deal with death.

Shortly after your beloved's death you wrote to me saying that you knew her soul was still alive:

> I knew, in a way I had never known anything before, that she was more alive than she had ever been. Even during my darkest hours, when grief made my life nearly unbearable, I never wished to bring her back, not if it

meant she would ever have to suffer again. I have to admit, though, that I sometimes begged God to take my life. For the first time, I think, I know something of what Paul might have felt when he wrote, "I desire to depart and be with Christ, which is better by far" (Philippians 1:23).

When I read those words, Jean, I couldn't help thinking that your confidence in your beloved's immortality was well justified. Jesus said, "I am the resurrection and the life. He who believes in me will live, even though he dies" (John 11:25).

Although none of us knows exactly what happens at the moment of death, both Scripture and experience give us every reason to believe that all is well.

When I was a young man in my first pastorate, I had the honor of ministering to a wonderful Christian lady as she faced death. She was suffering from a fatal illness, and as she grew physically weaker, I could not help but notice how her thoughts turned more and more toward heaven. As the moment of her death drew near, she fixed her attention on the opposite side of the room, and the most peaceful expression settled on her countenance. Just before she drew her last breath, she said in a voice barely audible, "Jesus. I see Jesus."

Now if this were an isolated incident, it would be comforting, but not necessarily conclusive. But it is not an isolated incident. Scripture and experience combine to testify to the fact that there is life after death. Taken together, they constitute an impressive witness and continuing source of encouragement.

Stephen, the first Christian martyr, cried out as he was being stoned: "Look," he said, "I see heaven open and the Son of Man standing at the right hand of God" (Acts 7:56).

In his book, *Facing Death and the Life After,* Billy Graham relates a similar testimony from his wife, Ruth, who recently died:

> Ruth tells about an experience she had in China. In the place where she lived, one of the evangelistic missionaries was Ad Talbot, whom she affectionately called Uncle Ad. Talbot had five sons and a daughter, Margaret Gay, a girl he deeply loved. Sometime after the beloved daughter's death, he was in the country with a Chinese Christian woman who was dying. As he knelt beside her bed, the old woman's face lit up and she said to Uncle Ad, "I see heaven, and Jesus is on the right hand of God, and Margaret Gay is with him." At that moment the room was filled with heavenly music and the Chinese woman was dead.

As you know, Jean, Christianity teaches that at the instant of death, our new life begins. The moment we take our final breath on earth, we take our first breath in heaven. Our bodies are placed in the grave to await the resurrection, but our spirits are immediately present with the Lord.

A seminary professor once remarked, "Most people dread death, but personally, I am not afraid to die, though I don't court death. . . . Christians face death with faith, believing that it opens the door to a land of goodness and gladness." Sudden death means sudden glory. Think of the thrill the believer will feel upon arriving home, as you read this poem by Herbert Lockyer in The Funeral Sourcebook.

> Think of stepping on shore,
> And finding it heaven!
> Think of taking hold of a hand,
> And finding it God's hand!
>
> Think of breathing a new air
> And finding it celestial air!
> Of feeling invigorated,
> And finding it immortality!
> Of passing from storm and tempest into perfect calm!
> Of awaking and knowing—
> I am home!

When your beloved died, her spirit went immediately to be with the Lord. Yet her redemption is not complete, and will not be, until she receives her glorified body at the second coming of Jesus Christ. Now she eagerly awaits the redemption of her body (Romans 8:23). Consider her death like the planting of a seed: "When you sow, you do not plant the body that will be, but just a seed.... The body that is sown is perishable, it is raised imperishable; it is sown in dishonor, it is raised in glory; it is sown in weakness, it is raised in power; it is sown a natural body, it is raised a spiritual body" (1 Corinthians 15:37, 42–44).

The question before us then is not, "Is there life after death?" That's a scriptural certainty! But rather, "What is the nature of that life?" What we want to know is, "How are the dead raised? With what kind of body will they come?" (1 Corinthians 15:35).

Most of our questions regarding the details of eternal life will probably go unanswered. The reality of our immortality is simply beyond us. We have no frame of reference and nothing to which we can compare it. Any earthly thing God might use as a way of comparison would diminish the glories of heaven at least as much as it revealed them. As a consequence, most attempts to describe heaven are little more than exercises in futility.

Anyone who has ever seriously tried to describe this eternal realm knows something of Apostle Paul's frustration. He wrote, "Fourteen years ago I was taken up to heaven for a visit. Don't ask me whether my body was there or just my spirit, for I don't know; only God can answer that. But anyway, there I was in paradise, and heard things so astounding that they are beyond a man's power to describe or put in words (and anyway I am not allowed to tell them to others)" (2 Corinthians 12:2–4 TLB).

Given that truth, perhaps the place to start is not with heaven, but with our glorified bodies. If we can come to some understanding of what they will be like, then maybe we can imagine, at least in some small way, the glories of heaven. Since our resurrected bodies will be fashioned after our Lord's glorious body, which is mentioned in Philippians 3:21, we need look no further than the risen Jesus to see what they will be like.

The first thing one notices about Jesus following His resurrection is that His appearance is so "human." Although He has a spiritual body, it is composed of flesh and bone. The disciples could see Him with their natural eyes, and they could touch Him with their natural hands. When He appeared to them following His resurrection, He said, "Look at my hands and my feet. It is I myself! Touch me and see; a ghost does not have flesh and bones, as you see I have" (Luke 24:39).

In fact, Jesus' appearance was so "ordinary" that on that first Easter morning, Mary Magdalene mistook Him for the gardener (John 20:10–16). And later that same day, two disillusioned disciples journeyed with Him from Jerusalem to Emmaus without recognizing Him. They thought He was just another weary traveler (Luke 24:13–35).

On more than one occasion after His resurrection, Jesus enjoyed a meal with His friends. The first time He appeared to His disciples, He asked them, "'Do you have anything here to eat?' They gave him a piece of broiled fish, and he took it and ate it in their presence" (Luke 24:41–43). On another occasion He surprised the weary disciples by preparing breakfast for them on the beach following a long night of fishing (John 21:1–14).

Yet, for all that, Jesus' resurrected body was no ordinary body. He was not limited by time or space but appeared and disappeared at will. He would suddenly materialize in the presence of those who believed in Him and just as suddenly disappear, only to reappear someplace else. In truth, His resurrected body had all the advantages of this natural body but none of its limitations. And since our mortal bodies will be transformed into the likeness of His glorious body, we, too, can expect to enjoy the same freedom from the limits of time and space.

I would like to think, Jean, that in heaven we will be able to work without becoming weary; that we will be able to love without being jealous or possessive; that we will be able to enjoy relationships without misunderstanding; that we will be able to worship fully and uninhibitedly; and that we will be able, finally, to know God completely—even as He knows us.

In heaven, singers will sing as they have never sung before. Composers will compose new music on a scale heretofore unknown. Creative geniuses will continue to invent. Gifted craftsmen will design and build things their natural minds couldn't even conceive. Writers will write and preachers will preach—but in that glorious realm everything will be done to a degree never imagined by mortal man.

Now look what I've done. I've allowed myself to be drawn into the very trap I was determined to avoid—using earthly comparisons in an attempt to describe heaven's eternal glories. It simply will not work because, "No eye has seen, no ear has heard, no mind has conceived what God has prepared for those who love him" (1 Corinthians 2:9).

Jean, although we cannot conceive of heaven's glories, the promise of eternal life nonetheless provides an undeniable strength in the time of loss, as well as an unwavering hope for the future. It does not eliminate the pain of our grief, but it does put it into perspective. Let me illustrate.

Some years ago my brother and his family left the United States to become missionaries in Argentina. For them, it was the fulfillment of a lifelong dream. For the rest of us it was a painfully blessed moment. We were happy for Joel and his family. He had prepared his entire life for this moment. We knew that he would be happier in Argentina, that this work was what he was destined to do. Still, we were nearly overwhelmed with our grief. All we could think about were the thousands of miles that would separate us, the four years we would be apart. Try as we might, we could not hold back our tears.

With a determined effort, we reminded ourselves that this separation, painful though it was, was only temporary. All of us would be reunited in the not-too-distant future. Without question, that was a comfort to us as we said our good-byes, but it did not fill the emptiness we felt as Joel and his family boarded that huge jet plane, nor did it stop our tears. Yet, even as we cried, we were also rejoicing.

That's how believers grieve when a loved one dies. We are not without hope; nor are we fatalistic, as those who have no assurance of eternal life are; but still there are tears, for death creates a great void in the lives of those who are left behind. In truth, we celebrate eternal life with a tear in our eye.

For departed believers, death is not the end of life; rather, it is simply the end of sin, sorrow, and suffering. Their lives continue, and your beloved's life continues, on a scale we cannot imagine: "And I heard a loud voice from the throne saying, 'Now the dwelling of God is with men, and he will live with them. They will be his people, and God himself will be with them and be their God. He will wipe every tear from their eyes. There will be no more death or mourning or crying or pain, for the old order of things has passed away'" (Revelation 21:3-4).

Jean, we both know that your beloved is with Jesus. She is more alive now than she has ever been. Still, that does not mean that you should not grieve. Yet, even in the midst of your grief, you can find comfort in the promise of an eternal reunion. In eternity you will be reunited with your beloved; you will renew your relationship on a higher level than any you ever experienced here.

I say that based on what both Scripture and reason reveal about life after death. Although the ultimate reality of heaven is beyond our comprehension, God has revealed the essence of it. And always that essence is of a far grander scale than anything this earthly life affords. That being the case, how can we doubt that our most intimate earthly relationships will not be enhanced in heaven? I agree with C. S. Lewis, who said, "I think the union between the risen spouses will be as close as that between the soul and its own risen body."

Jean, take hope. The best is yet to come!

In His comfort,
Richard

Lord Jesus, You are the resurrection and the life! You have conquered death, hell, and the grave. You have prepared an eternal abode for Your own and already my beloved is with You. She is more alive now than she has ever been. Although my loneliness is unspeakable, I would not bring her back for anything. As much as I love her, I know You love her more. As happy as she was with me, I know she is even happier being with You. I take strength from Your abiding presence and comfort from Your promise of eternal life. One day my beloved and I will be together with You forever. Life without end! May Your name be glorified now and forever. Amen.

Epilogue
Telling Daddy Good-bye

In November 2006, my 83-year-old father fell and broke his hip. Subsequently, he underwent surgery and several weeks of rehabilitation before being released to our care. My sister turned the office in her home into a sick room, and all of us children chipped in to purchase a queen-size adjustable bed so Mother could continue to sleep with Daddy.

This was just the latest in a series of health Crisis that had beset my father. For 22 years he had battled heart disease—undergoing two open-heart surgeries—and fibrosis of the lungs. With a tenacity born of love and desperation, my mother and my sister took Dad from one doctor to another, always hoping for a magical cure. While the doctors were sympathetic, there wasn't really anything they could do except try to make Dad as comfortable as possible. In time he seemed to make peace with his situation, finding joy in reading and playing table games with Mother, but it wasn't much of a way to live. On more than one occasion he told me that if it wasn't for leaving Mom, he would welcome death. He wasn't being morbid; he was simply tired of suffering and homesick for heaven.

By the new year, it had become apparent that Dad was dying, although neither my sister nor my mother could bring themselves to admit it. The thought of losing him was simply more than they could bear. In late January, the doctors confirmed what we could no longer deny, telling us that our father had only two to four weeks to live. When my sister broke the news to Dad, a small smile touched his lips, and he said, "Well, they've finally given me some good news."

Soon all the children, grandchildren, and even the great-grandchildren gathered at my sister's home, and on Thursday afternoon, February 8, 2007, my father departed this world. His home-going was peaceful, although the weeks preceding it were filled with considerable suffering. He bore it all with remarkable grace—the pain and choking, the inability to eat and the humiliation of not being able to care for himself. As the end drew near, he became ever more affectionate, repeatedly kissing and hugging those of us who cared for him.

The last Sunday before his death we all crowded around his bed for worship. For the most part Dad seemed oblivious, but when it came time to receive Communion, he opened his eyes and reached for the cup and the bread. Kneeling beside his bed, I took his hand and began to quote John 14:2–3 (KJV). As I said the familiar words, "In my Father's house are many mansions …" he moved his lips, soundlessly mouthing the words along with me. As we sang his favorite hymns, he seemed to draw strength from them. Not strength to live but the strength to pass from this life to the next without fear.

Two days later he fell into a coma from which he awakened only momentarily at the very end. Mother was lying on the bed beside him, as was my sister. My brothers were at his bedside: Stanley was standing at the head of the bed, softly stroking Daddy's hair, while Joel was standing beside him, holding Daddy's hand. Standing between them and just a little behind, I had a clear view of my father's face. For days he had lain with his head back and his mouth wide open as he labored to breathe, but as he drew his last breath, he closed his mouth and opened his eyes. Focusing on something only he could see, Daddy smiled and tried to sit up, and then he was gone.

Thinking about it now, I am sure Jesus came for Dad just as He promised He would: "If I go and prepare a place for you, I will come again, and receive you unto myself; that where I am, there ye may be also" (John 14:3 KJV). There was no death angel in that room, just the Lord of life coming to call my father to his eternal reward.

The images of the last days I spent with my father have been forever etched upon my heart. One of the many things I will never forget is the memory of the love and devotion heaped upon him by his family and friends. It was a rare and special thing, and I can only conclude that the man or woman who goes into eternity loved like that is rich indeed.

The funeral service was deeply moving, filled with memories of the past and hope for the future. No one captured the hope of eternal life more powerfully than my brother Joel. Having spent nearly all of his adult life serving as a missionary in Latin America, he understands what it means to be a pilgrim and a stranger in a foreign land. When it was his turn to speak, he said, "For the past 30 years I have been required to carry official documents identifying me as a 'resident alien.' Although I drink *mate* like an Argentine, eat *asado* with the best of them, and speak the language as if it were my mother tongue, I am still a 'resident alien,' and I always will be. I love Argentina and its people, but I will never be an Argentine. I am an American, and America will always be my home."

Pausing to collect himself he continued, "When we went to the mission field in 1976, we were truly cut off from our families and our homeland. After four long years we flew home for our first furlough. When we landed at Miami International Airport, I spotted a U.S. Postal Service mail box and began to weep. I know that must seem silly to you, but it symbolized home to me, and I was overcome with emotion. In the ensuing years we have passed through customs scores of times upon our return to the United States; still each time we do, Martine eagerly waits for the immigration official to stamp her passport and then look up and say, 'Welcome home.'"

Struggling to control his emotions, he said, "When Daddy took his last breath, I knew I had lost an irretrievable part of myself. The man who gave me life was gone, and it felt like I had a hole in my heart. On another level, I rejoiced because I knew Daddy was more alive than he had ever been, and even as I wept with grief, I rejoiced for him. With the eye of faith, I saw Daddy getting his passport stamped at heaven's gate. I could almost hear Jesus say, 'Welcome home, Dick Exley! Welcome home.'"

It gives me great joy to recall Joel's words, and more especially to know that Dad is no longer a "resident alien" in this world of pain, but a full-fledged citizen of heaven and a member of that great cloud of witnesses (Hebrews 12:1). Of course, this does not eliminate the pain of our loss, but it does put it into perspective. Even as we grieve, we are comforted with the knowledge that one day we will be reunited never to part.

Good-bye, Daddy. I will always love you. In life you taught me how to live, and in death you have shown me how to die with dignity. Your fingerprints are all over my life, and I will always be in your debt.

God's Peace, My Peace

trusting

God in

terrifying

times

An activity for children who experienced
the earthquake, led by parents and other
adults who love children

Given free to the Children of Haiti by

David C Cook

This is an activity to help children who have been through the earthquake trust in God and allow him to help them replace their fears with peace. Begin by reading the whole activity. Then decide if you will use it with your own children or with a group of children, perhaps in a Sunday school setting.

You have permission from David C. Cook to make copies of this activity lesson and the craft project. You do not need additional permission. Copies must be given away free.

Directions and Preparation for Adults

- This is an activity that teaches children to trust God when bad things happen. God has promised to love us forever, and he will keep on loving us even when our world is falling apart.

- You can use this activity with a large group of children in a church or school or orphanage. As a parent, you can use this at home with your own child.

- The activity has four parts. Children learn by doing, so as they are going through this activity, they will be active and involved.

- You will need to make preparations for some parts of this activity. Read everything carefully and be sure you allow enough time to prepare the materials you need. (If you are a parent using this at home, ask your children to help with the preparations.)

- After describing the preparations, you will be guided through the whole activity. These sheets will tell you what to do, what to say, and what questions to ask the children. Read this in advance, so you're very familiar with it. The parts that you will read or say directly to the children are printed in bold, dark green type. Of course you don't have to say everything word for word. Make it natural for you.

- When you start talking about these things, your children may have serious questions, especially if they're older. They may wonder why God let their friends or relatives die. They may have questions about heaven. Answer these questions to the best of your ability, but don't fake it. There are many things we don't understand about God. It's all right to admit that. This activity doesn't try to explain everything. It focuses on the simple but valuable truth that God loves us and provides peace to our lives in times of trouble.

- The first preparation: prayer. Take some time to pray for God's strength and guidance for yourself as you lead this activity. And ask for his peace. Pray for each child you'll be leading. Ask God to speak his message into their hearts.

Parts of this Activity

1. "What does fear look like?" (No materials needed.)

2. The prayer walk. (Materials needed for the walkway and prayer stations. See opposite page.)

3. Craft: Wings of prayer. (Cut out materials based on the model included here.)

4. Passing the peace. (No materials needed.)

Preparations for the Prayer Walk

The Prayer Walk sets up six different "stations" where children go to think about, and to pray about, their feelings. You will need to make certain decisions before you start to set it up.

Where will children walk?

If you are doing this at home or in a temporary living space, children don't really need to walk at all. You could place the six stations in different parts of the same space and just turn your attention from one station to the next.

It is possible to do the Prayer Walk outside, to map out a route *around* your home or *through* your neighborhood. The only problem with this is *distraction.* Will the children be able to focus on their praying with a lot of outdoor activity around them?

If you're in a school or church, you could easily do the Prayer Walk in one room or along a hallway, or you could put stations in different classrooms.

How will the children be led through the Prayer Walk?

If you are doing the lesson with just one or a few children, it's easy. Lead them to the various stations yourself. Give them the instructions at each station and allow time for them to do the activity.

If you are teaching a larger class of children, you have several options.

(A) If the children are good readers, post the instructions at each station and send the children through the Prayer Walk on their own. (One advantage to this is that each child can go at his or her own pace.)

(B) You could divide the class into small groups and lead one group through the Prayer Walk at a time, while the others work on the "Wings of Prayer."

(C) You could put a different adult leader at each of the stations to give instructions as the children go through.

(D) This would require some electronic equipment, but you could pre-record all the instructions in order. Provide a couple of tape players with headphones and let the children go through the Prayer Walk one by one, pressing PLAY as they get to each new station. (You'll be working on the "Wings of Prayer" with the other children.)

What will happen at each station on the Prayer Walk?

Station 1

You'll need marbles or pebbles, one for each child, and a clear glass or bowl filled with water. The Scripture text for this station is Psalms 46:1-7. (If children are going through the Prayer Walk by themselves, have that text available to them in a printout or open Bible.)

Station 2

You'll need pieces of paper, one for each child, and pencils, pens, crayons, or charcoal. (Children will be drawing.) Also, a wastebasket. The text is Psalms 103:8-12. (Again, if children are going through the Pray Walk by themselves, have this text available to them in a printout or open Bible.)

Station 3

You'll need copies of a "prayer card," one for each child. Write the following text on it. If children can't write, give each child a blank card. Read the text to them twice. Ask them to draw a picture that will remind them of what you read.

Jesus is always with me.
Jesus loves me.
Jesus walks beside me
to comfort me when I am sad or afraid.

Jesus will never leave me.
He loves me and wants me to trust him.
Jesus is my friend
who is always here when I am sad or afraid.

Station 4

You'll need a bunch of grapes, with one for each child. (Other food could be substituted if necessary, but some sort of fruit would be best.)

Station 5

You'll need a small container of scented oil, or some other fragrant substance. (Just make sure it's safe for children.)

Station 6

You'll need a small mirror. The Scripture text is Micah 6:8.

How do you get ready to help children make "Wings of Prayer?"

Have copies of the Wings of Prayer worksheet, one for each child. You could trace copies onto white paper. You'll need scissors and glue. You might also want crayons.

THE ACTIVITY

Part 1: What does fear look like?

- Have you ever been afraid? When were you afraid? What was happening?

- What were you afraid of?

- What do people look like when they get scared?

Sometimes, though, people get scared and they don't scream or jump. They don't show it at all. But deep inside, they're worried about things that might happen or something bad will happen again. This worry can put them in a bad mood, or it can give them bad dreams.

- Do you ever worry about things?

- What do you feel like inside when you worry?

God has a special message for us when we feel afraid or when we worry. We find it in Isaiah chapter 41.

Read, or have a capable student read, Isaiah 41:10.

So don't worry, because I am with you.
Don't be afraid, because I am your God.
I will make you strong and will help you;
I will support you with my right hand that saves you.

(New Century Version)

God knows that we will be frightened, but he tells us not to worry. Why? Because he is with us. He says he will help us, he will make us strong. And when we trust in Jesus, even death doesn't have to be a scary thing, because we know we will live forever in heaven.

- What does the word *peace* mean?

- How do you feel inside when you are peaceful?

The Bible says that God will give us peace if we ask him. It's a peace that we can never totally understand. With God's peace, even when our world is falling apart and is scary, we know that God is with us.

How do we get this peace? We find this peace in Jesus. We get it when we talk with him—praying and also listening, reading his words and telling him how we feel.

We can do all of these things in the Prayer Walk.

Part 2: The Prayer Walk

I have set up six different places where you can talk with God in different ways. This will be fun, but it's also serious. It's a time when you can tell God exactly how you've been feeling lately, and maybe you will even begin to feel a little bit better.

You won't have to walk very far to get to these stations, but I want you to imagine that you're taking a long hike. Close your eyes right now and imagine this with me. See yourself walking. What's around you? Busy city streets? Or are you climbing the mountains? Can you see the ocean? Or are you looking at grassy fields, or farmland? No matter where you go, God is with you. He will meet you there.

So with those pictures fresh in our minds, let's go to the first station.

NOTE: Adjust the following instructions as needed, depending on the materials available.

Station 1

You'll need marbles or pebbles, one for each child, and a clear glass or bowl filled with water. The Scripture text for this station is Psalm 46:1-7. (If children are going through the Prayer Walk by themselves, have that text available to them in a printout or open Bible.)

Take off your shoes. Take a deep breath and let it out slowly. Imagine yourself playing in the gentle waves. Pick up a pebble [or marble] from the pile. Hold it in your hand. Make it your "worry pebble." Give it a worry name. What have you been worrying about? Well, that's the name of your worry pebble. Now offer your worry to God. Let God take care of whatever that worry is. And drop your worry pebble into the bowl of water. The water is like God's love. It surrounds our worries so we can let them go. God doesn't want us to worry about things we have no control over.

When you start worrying about things, it's like stepping on a sharp stone. It bothers you with every step you take. Stop and get rid of your worry by dropping it into God's ocean of love.

Listen to what the Bible says in Psalm 46.

God is our protection and our strength.
*   He always helps in times of trouble.*
So we will not be afraid even if the earth shakes,
*   or the mountains fall into the sea,*
even if the oceans roar and foam,
*   or the mountains shake at the raging sea.*

The Lord All-Powerful is with us;
*   the God of Jacob is our defender.*

Let's move on to Station 2.

Station 2

You'll need pieces of paper, one for each child, and pencils, pens, crayons, or charcoal. (Children will be drawing.) Also, a wastebasket. The text is Psalm 103:8-12. (Again, if children are going through the Prayer Walk by themselves, have this text available to them in a printout or open Bible.)

Imagine you're climbing on a cement rock pile. You really have to strain your legs. You almost twist your ankle. This is tough. You worry about falling.

Sometimes we do things that make us worry. Maybe we hurt somebody, or did something that God didn't like. We feel sad about that, and we hope God will forgive us.

Here at this station, pick up a piece of paper and something to draw with. Draw on the paper a hurt you want God to forgive. Did you take something that wasn't yours? Did you cheat or lie? Are you feeling guilty about it now? Then draw it out on the paper. It doesn't have to be an artistic masterpiece. It's just a way of telling God what you did.

Do you know what it means to *confess* our sin? It means telling God we're sorry. It means asking him to forgive us. Do that right now. Whatever you drew on the paper, tell God you're sorry for it.

(Allow time for this.)

The beautiful thing is that God says he will forgive our sins. He forgets about them. So take your paper and tear it in half. Then tear those pieces in half again. And again. Crush the paper into a small ball. Then throw it in the trash can.

Listen to what the Bible says in Psalm 52: 103 (New Century Version).

The Lord shows mercy and is kind.
> *He does not become angry quickly, and he has great love.*
He will not always accuse us,
> *and he will not be angry forever.*
He has not punished us as our sins should be punished;
> *he has not repaid us for the evil we have done.*
As high as the sky is above the earth,
> *so great is his love for those who respect him.*
He has taken our sins away from us
> *as far as the east is from west.*

Let's move on to Station 3.

Station 3

In this part of our journey, it doesn't matter where we're walking. The main thing is *who is walking beside us.* Imagine yourself with a good friend, with someone who loves you very much. Someone who makes you happy, someone who lights up the journey and makes the walk easier. This "someone" is Jesus.

He is the light of the world. Close your eyes and remember how he calmed the storm, how he healed the sick, how he welcomed children into his arms. Jesus knows you by name. He loved you enough to give his life for you. Jesus was there at the creation of the world. In fact, the Bible says that Jesus is a kind of glue that holds the whole universe together. He is God's own Son, our Savior.

He is the all-powerful God, and he is our friend. That gives us hope for every part of life. We don't need to worry, because Jesus is walking with us.

Now take a Prayer Card and read this poem by yourself, slowly. Think about Jesus walking beside you.

You'll need copies of a "prayer card," one for each child. Write the full text of "Christ be with me" on it. If children can't write, give each child a blank card. Read the text to them twice. Ask them to draw a picture that reminds them of what you read.

Jesus is always with me.
Jesus loves me.
Jesus walks beside me
to comfort me when I am sad or afraid.

Jesus will never leave me.
He loves me and wants me to trust him.
Jesus is my friend
who is always here when I am sad or afraid.

Keep this card with you, and pull it out whenever you begin to be afraid. It will remind you that Jesus Christ is always with you.

Let's move on to Station 4.

Station 4

You'll need a bunch of grapes, with one for each child. (Other food could be substituted if necessary, but some sort of fruit would be best.)

Where is our walk taking us now? Imagine that we're out in the fields. Crops are growing all around us. There are trees and vines that produce their fruit.

Jesus often talked with his disciples about food and crops and the process of growing. He told them that he was like the trunk of the tree, and they were like the branches. The Bible also says that we produce fruit, just like a grape vine or a fruit tree. God's power is with us, inside of us, and he helps us to do and say good things. So take this piece of fruit in your hand, but don't eat it yet. Hear the voice of Jesus saying to you, "I gave my life for you, so that you might lead a delicious life."

Now eat the fruit, and hear the voice of Jesus saying, "I will be with you always. Whenever you have something to do, and you're not sure you can do it, ask for my help. With my help, you can produce good fruit."

Thank Jesus for his help, and then let's move on to Station 5.

Station 5

You'll need a small container of scented oil, or some other fragrant substance. (Just make sure it's safe for children.)

Imagine yourself walking up the steps to a great palace. This is more beautiful than the greatest palace you have ever seen, greater even than the president's palace was before the earthquake. You are going to a party that the King of the Universe is throwing for a special guest. You come into the main hall and the King welcomes you personally. You are his special guest.

He tells you to sit here in this place of honor. In Bible times, people honored special guests by anointing them with oil. Priests used special, great-smelling oil to mark things that were set apart for God's use. So let's

do that here. Take some of this fragrant oil on your finger and rub it on the back of your hand. Smell the oil on your hand. God's presence in your life is soothing, like it is a wonderful smell. You are set apart as his special child. God loves you and cares for you.

Bad things will happen in this world. Some things will make us cry. Some things will scare us. But remember that you are still God's special guest. He loves you, no matter what happens. Now put another dab of oil on your finger and use it to draw a heart on the palm of your hand. Breathe the warm smell again. Thank God for surrounding you with his love.

Now let's move on to the last station, Station 6.

Station 6

You'll need a small mirror. The Scripture text is Micah 6:8.

Imagine yourself walking to your favorite place, wherever that is. Jesus is walking with you. Maybe he even carries you on his shoulders for a while. But now imagine that other people are there too, all around you. How does Jesus want you to treat them? With the same love he shows to you.

Pick up the mirror and look at it. What do you see? It's your image.

The Bible says that the more we talk with Jesus, the more we become like him. We become sort of a mirror-image of him. So when he shows love to us, we show love to others. When he helps us, we help others. When he calms our fears, we can try to calm our friends and family when they are afraid.

Hear what God's prophet says in Micah 6:8.

> The Lord has told you . . . what he wants from you:
> to do what is right to other people,
> love being kind to others,
> and live humbly, obeying your God.

Take some time right now to talk with God about the people you know who might be hurting and scared. Ask him to help those in need. See if he wants you to help him do that.

And now we walk back into the place where we live, but we don't leave Jesus behind. No, he keeps walking with us wherever we go.

Part 3: Wings of Prayer

God invites us to pray to him about anything. When we're troubled or concerned or afraid, we can pray and tell him about our feelings. You might think of your prayer like a bird that flies up from you toward God. To help us remember that every prayer we pray flies up to God, we're going to make a "prayer bird." Every time you see your "prayer bird," you'll be reminded to talk to God.

Hand each child one of the Wings of Prayer birds. The pattern is at the end of this lesson.

1. Use scissors to cut out the rectangular base and the dove figure.

2. Have each child write his or her name on the line in the rectangular base.

What are you concerned about? What are you praying for? Before we start putting the bird together, turn over the base (where you just wrote your name) and write a simple prayer. Or if you prefer, draw a little picture of something you're praying about.

3. Children should fold the bird in half, and then fold the wings up and fold the tail out on the dotted lines. (If you want children to color or decorate the birds, they can do that now.)

4. Now they should glue the folded tail pieces to the space marked on the base.

There it is. Every time you look at your Wings of Prayer, remember that your prayers always wing themselves up to God. You know he hears everything you say to him and he cares deeply.

Part 4: Passing the Peace

• What will you remember from today's experience?

• What was your favorite part?

Let's close today with a practice that Christians have been doing for a very long time. It's called, passing the peace. I'll show you how it works:

Call a child to stand with you. Extend your hand and say: **The peace of Christ be with you.** *Instruct the child to respond,* **And also with you.**

If you're teaching multiple children, have them do the same thing with each other.

Haiti session written by Randy Petersen. Original session following the destruction of the New York City Towers on 9/11 was written by Mary Grace Becker and Lois Keffer. The Wings of Prayer is copyright © Lois Keffer and printed in Paper Capers by David C. Cook.

Design and illustration by Scott Johnson, BMB Design

Haitian Creole Translation by Jean Killick Aristide & Marie Nehemie Aristide

Reviewed for best practices in helping children deal with fear and trauma by Janet McCormack, D.Min., B.C.C. and Heather Davediuk Gingrich, Ph.D., both from Denver Seminary, Colorado U.S.A.

Resource expert: Dr. Dieumeme Noelliste, Vice Chairman of the Board of STEP (Seminary of Evangelical Theology of Port-au-Prince). He is professor of Theological Ethics, Denver Seminary.

Wings of Prayer

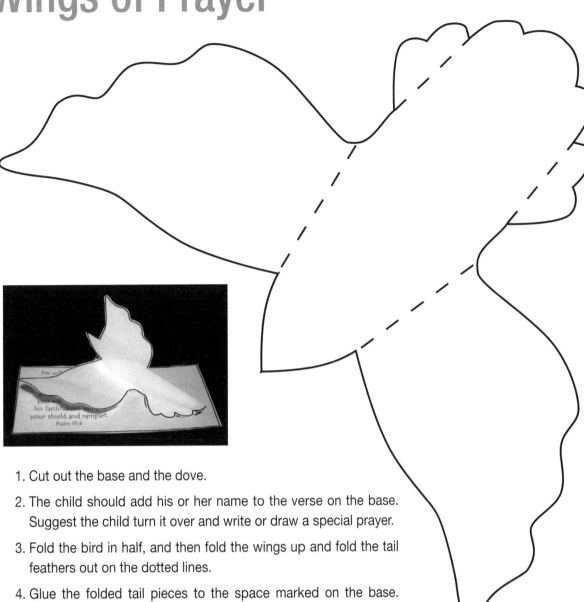

1. Cut out the base and the dove.

2. The child should add his or her name to the verse on the base. Suggest the child turn it over and write or draw a special prayer.

3. Fold the bird in half, and then fold the wings up and fold the tail feathers out on the dotted lines.

4. Glue the folded tail pieces to the space marked on the base. The bird will look like it is taking flight, just like children's prayers.

He will cover you,

_____,

with his feathers,
and under his wings
You can hide.
You will not fear.

Psalms 91:4, 5

Glue tail
pieces here.

Someone I Love Died

Written by
Christine H. Tangvald

Given to the
Children of Haiti by
David C Cook

SOMEONE I LOVE DIED
Published by David C. Cook
4050 Lee Vance View
Colorado Springs, CO 80918 U.S.A.

David C. Cook Distribution Canada
55 Woodslee Avenue, Paris, Ontario, Canada N3L 3E5

David C. Cook U.K., Kingsway Communications
Eastbourne, East Sussex BN23 6NT, England

David C. Cook and the graphic circle C logo
are registered trademarks of Cook Communications Ministries.

Written by Christine Harder Tangvald. Haiti edit by Mary Grace Becker

Design and illustration by Scott Johnson, BMB Design

Haitian Creole Translation by Jean Killick Aristide & Marie Nehemie Aristide

Reviewed for best practices in helping children deal with trauma by Janet McCormack, D.Min., B.C.C. and Heather Davediuk Gingrich, Ph.D., both from Denver Seminary, Colorado U.S.A.

Resource Expert: Dr. Dieumeme Noelliste, Vice Chairman of the Board of STEP (Seminary of Evangelical Theology of Port-au-Prince). The school in Port-au-Prince was destroyed in the earthquake and one student died. He is professor of Theological Ethics, Denver Seminary.

Scripture quotations, unless otherwise noted, are taken from the Holy Bible, New International Version®. Copyright ©1973, 1978, 1984 by International Bible Society. Used by permission of Zondervan. All rights reserved.

ISBN 978-1-5551-3490-7

First printing in this edition 2010

Printed in U.S.A.

Someone
I Love Died

Written by
Christine H. Tangvald

Someone I love died in the great earthquake in Haiti.

That person's name is _____.

I love _____ a lot.

Here is a picture I can draw of the person who died.

When a person dies, some people
think it is the end of things.
But they are wrong, aren't they?
That's not how God works.

God has a plan for everyone in this lovely
land of Haiti we call home.
A plan for life.
A plan for death.
And a plan for life after death.

Still . . . thinking about death is sad, isn't it?

**Draw how your face looks when you are
thinking about the person who died.**

Not long ago, the ground shook and buildings fell.
We quickly forgot about singing songs
and great big hugs and laughter.

We no longer went to school, or played football,
or said our prayers.
We thought God was mad at us.

There are lots of things about death—
and earthquakes—that are hard to understand.

To help us understand death a little better,

let's start at the beginning.

Did you know that a long time ago,

God created the body

for the very first man out of earth's dust?

He did.

Scoop up a handful of dirt and slowly release it.

Can you believe that God made

the first man out of dust?

How amazing!

God breathed into the man's body
the *breath of life* and
the man became a living person.
Genesis 2:7

God created people different from
cows and dogs and birds.
God created people special—
a lot like himself.

God created people in his own image.

1 2 3 4 5

6 7 8 9 10

Circle the number of very special people in your life.
Put a special person's name over each number.

Now, when one of God's people dies,
God lovingly moves the breath of life
from the body to a special place we call *heaven,*
a place we can't see right now.

A very important part of the person does not die…ever!
It's true. This is the part that we call the *soul*—
the part that lived inside the body—the part that
makes us laugh and cry and listen
and feel and pray and think.

That soul moves to heaven to live with Jesus
forever and ever and ever.

And not only that, but guess who loves it in heaven?
It's someone you know.

_____ does!
(Fill in the name of the person who died.)

Heaven is a wonderful place filled with *joy.*

Draw a picture of a day when you were happy.

While you draw, sing or hum a song that makes you smile inside,

even when it's hard to smile on the outside.

When a person dies, the body is like an empty house.
Nobody lives in it anymore.

And since the body isn't needed,
it is usually placed in the ground and covered with dirt.
It doesn't really matter where the empty body is,
because the soul has moved on
and is happy in heaven.

Understanding this is hard, but it's part of God's plan.

One question I have is:

For the person who died, it is the end of life on earth,

but it is the beginning of life in heaven.

It's a new beginning—much like a new birthday.

And just like our birthday is a happy day,

this person's birthday in heaven

is a very happy day, too.

Then . . . why aren't we happy?

Life just doesn't seem fair.

We want those who died in the earthquake

to come back to us.

We want things to be the way they were.

But that can't happen. It just can't.

So we are lonely.

We feel upset.

In fact, it's okay to feel any way you feel.

Some people feel sad or angry.

Some don't.

Some people feel lonely or scared.

Some don't.

Some people wish they had died with the person they loved
or even instead of that person.

And some people don't know exactly how they feel,
except that they are upset,
and nothing feels right anymore.

However you feel is okay. You might want to cry and cry.
Sometimes it feels good to cry.
Crying is another way to say, "I love you. I miss you."

How do you feel right now?

Have you ever tried to draw a feeling?

Maybe you can use sharp points or closed boxes

or a dark color to show that you hurt and are sad or mad.

Try to draw your feeling and then explain what

you have drawn to someone you trust.

It's good to remember that with God
all things are possible.
So, the next time you feel sad or lonely
say to yourself . . .

With time, I will feel better and be happy again.
Maybe I don't think so right now,
but it will happen.

Someday I won't feel so sad and lonely.
Someday I'll start to smile again and even laugh.

Maybe not right now, but later.

I will.

I might even play a game of marbles, hide-and-seek
or football with my friends.
I might jump rope or play mancala.
I might fly a kite.

Someday I will be happy again.

**Draw a picture of you doing something
that often makes you happy.**

It often helps to tell someone how you feel right now!
Who can you talk to when you're upset?

I can talk to _____ or _____,
to my friends, or pastor.

And it's especially good to talk to God.
We need to talk to God even if we don't really want to.
God understands. He understands we didn't
want someone we love to die.
We can tell God just how we feel . . .
right now.

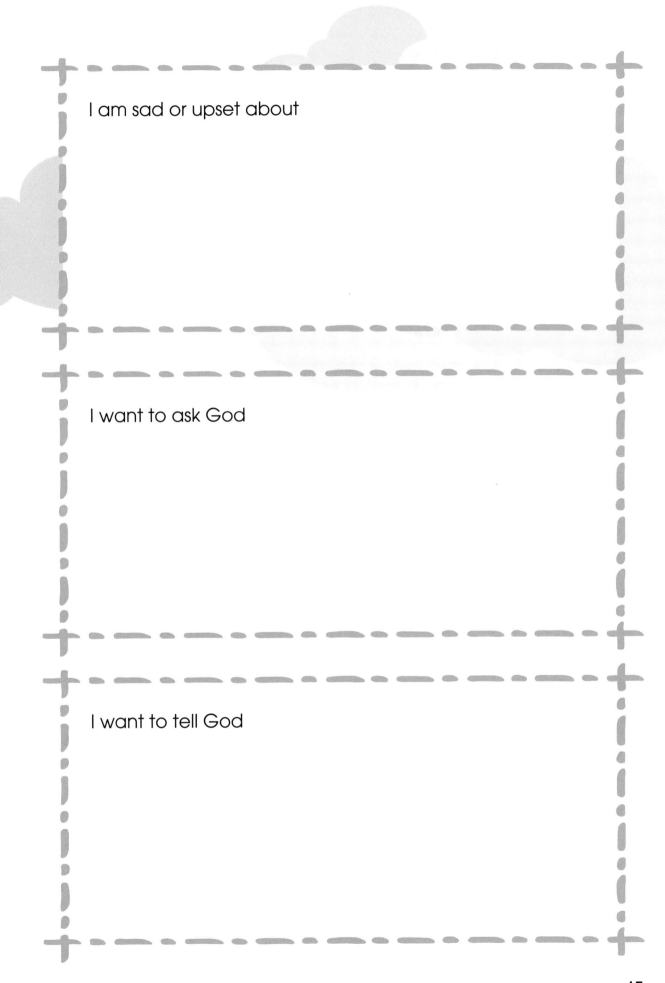

I am sad or upset about

I want to ask God

I want to tell God

Sometimes when we talk to God,
he gives us a calm,
quiet feeling called peace.

We feel safer and stronger
when we talk honestly with God.

He never gets angry when we tell him
we are mad or sad or scared.

He knows how we feel before we tell him.

Draw a picture of something beautiful in Haiti.

It could be a sunset or boats on the water

or anything you want to draw.

Did you ever wonder,
"How do people get to go to heaven?"

Oh, this is the best part of God's plan.
Jesus is the one who opens the door to heaven.
Jesus invites everyone in.

God sent his own Son, Jesus,
to show us how much he loves us.

Jesus lived here on earth.
Jesus died here on earth.
And Jesus was raised up from death.

Now he lives in heaven.
It is a miracle!

When we accept Jesus as our friend and Savior,

all our sins are forgiven, and he opens

the door for us to heaven.

And everyone is invited!

Jesus said, "I am the resurrection and the life.

He who believes in me will live,

even though he dies;

and whoever lives and believes in me will never die."

John 11:25; Ephesians 2:8.

Do you believe this?

Is Jesus your personal friend and Savior?

If your answer is yes, write a great big YES here.

Thank you, Jesus, for opening the door

to heaven for me and for _____,

the person I love who died.

Did you ever wonder,

"How fast does a person's soul go to heaven?"

Faster than you can clap your hands!

(Clap hands!)

Faster than you can stomp your feet!

(Stomp feet!)

Faster than you can say your name!

(Say your name!)

That is how fast the soul goes to heaven

when a person dies.

Even if the person's body cannot be found,

the soul goes to heaven right away.

Right away!

Jesus is waiting in heaven to welcome

everyone who loves him.

Do you ever wonder what heaven is like?
Are there stars in heaven, and flowers
and trees and animals and sunshine?
Does it rain in heaven? Will there be rainbows?

I hope so, don't you? But we really don't know.
We don't know exactly where heaven is or what it is like.
But we don't have to know, because God knows.

**Draw a picture of heaven as a joyous celebration
filled with your favorite kind of music.**

We don't know exactly what heaven is like.

But we do know that heaven is wonderful.

It is not a sad or scary place to be.

It is a happy place, a fun place, a wonderful place.

In fact, heaven is better than

the very best place you can think of.

Jesus said so.

He said, "In my Father's house are many rooms . . .

I am going there to prepare a place for you."

John 14:2.

We can trust Jesus' promise because Jesus never lies.

Never! Ever!

Heaven is one of the best parts of God's plan.

Lots of people already live in heaven.
You probably know some of them.

Can you write their names here?
Include the person who just died in the earthquake
and others you know who have died.

Lots of people from the Bible are in heaven, too.

Abraham and Moses

Matthew, Mark, Luke, and John

Mary and Martha

And there are angels in heaven.

There certainly are.

Lots of them!

Use your imagination to draw an angel here.

Just think! The person you love who is in heaven with Jesus

knows exactly what angels look like.

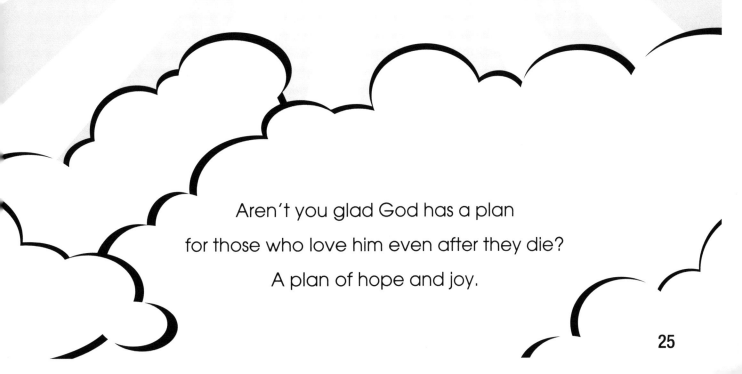

Aren't you glad God has a plan

for those who love him even after they die?

A plan of hope and joy.

Here some things to remember.

Draw a star in front of those things you want to make sure you remember.

☐ It's not my fault if someone dies.

☐ It's okay to feel however I feel.

☐ The person who died is just fine. The soul moved out of the body to special place called heaven.

☐ Jesus opens the door to heaven and everyone who loves him is invited in.

☐ Heaven is not a sad or scary place.
Heaven is wonderful . . . a place of joy. Jesus said so!

☐ God will help me through the sad and hard times, and sometime later I will feel happy again.

☐ Someday, all God's people will meet with Jesus in heaven. That will be a happy, happy day!

Thank you, God, for your perfect plan.

Prayer

Dear God,

Hi, it's me, _____ from Haiti.

Thank you for your plan, God.

Thank you for life on earth and life in heaven.

Thank you for making heaven safe and happy

so I don't have to worry.

God, I want to feel safe and happy here, too.

Please help me when I'm sad or wake up crying.

Help me when I'm lonely or mad, too.

I'm so glad to know I will feel better again—after a while.

Thank you, Jesus, for being my very own friend and Savior.

Thank you for opening the door to heaven.

You are the most important part of God's plan—and mine!

Knowing about this make me feel better.

But when I have more questions and mixed-up feelings,

I will be talking to you again, God.

Amen.

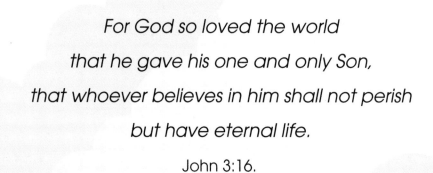

For God so loved the world
that he gave his one and only Son,
that whoever believes in him shall not perish
but have eternal life.

John 3:16.